23 Sept. 1993

DESKFORD PARISH

to my wife, Ray,

whose advice has so often saved me

"frae monie a blunder and foolish notion"

Cover picture...

An archaeological reconstruction of a carnyx, a Pictish war trumpet 1.5m long, based on the bronze boar's head carnyx dug up at Leitchestown farm, Deskford, Banffshire in 1816. This discovery, the finest example of six carnyx fragments existing in Europe's history, has been dated at AD 100-300.

Described as, **"this magnificent beast"**, by Fraser Hunter, Department of Archaeology, National Museums of Scotland.

DESKFORD PARISH

loons, lairds, preachers & teachers

George Anderson Clarke

winner of the

BRUCE HENDERSON MEMORIAL AWARD 1992

of the

ABERDEEN AND NORTH EAST SCOTLAND FAMILY HISTORY SOCIETY

First published September 1993

by the

ABERDEEN AND NORTH EAST SCOTLAND FAMILY HISTORY SOCIETY

The Family History Shop, 164 King Street, Aberdeen AB2 3BD

ISBN 0-947659-18-8

Printed in Scotland

by the

University of Stirling

Stirling FK9 4LA Scotland

Contents

Illustrations

Unattributed illustrations are by the author

about the author...

Born in 1924, from farming forebears in Rathven in the 1600s, who moved to Deskford in 1771.

Educated in Deskford (Dux of 1938) and at Buckie High School.

World War II: A flight engineer on Halifax bombers, serving in India and Burma.
After the war, a cartographic surveyor with the Ordnance Survey.

Gateshead Borough Councillor 1954-57. From 1957 a full-time trade union studies tutor and courses administrator with the National Council of Labour Colleges and, from 1965 to 1985, with the TUC Training College in London.

Preface

This account of a Deskert loon and his parents in the *Hungry Thirties*, and a longer look at the parish where they lived, is an extract from a projected history of the Clarkes of Rathven and Deskford, and their descendants in Australia, Canada, Israel, the U.S.A., and where else before I give up searching?

Like countless other Scots, after the war, I went to work in England, for forty long years. After retirement, my wife and I came to live in Stirling. Later, when re-visiting Deskford, my Brother John showed us copies of two letters, written one hundred years apart. The first, in 1885 by our Father, aged 13, to his Uncle, Capt. John Clarke in Quebec. The second, in 1985 from a hitherto unknown Cousin, the Rt Rev Jacob James Joseph Barclay, Bishop of East Jerusalem.

These two letters inspired me to start tracing my ancestors - *hunting deid folk*, my Wife disdainfully calls it. I joined the Aberdeen and North East Scotland Family History Society; in a few months I had family links back to 1694. My ancestors had farmed Mid Skeith and Hoggie, each for 150 years.

Soon, I was writing to new-found relatives in Israel, Canada, the U.S.A. and more recently, to a new-found, 77 year-old Cousin, the Grand-daughter of my Grand uncle, Dr William Clarke who emigrated from Deskford to Australia in 1879. I made this contact through a free ad in the *Western Australian*.

After compiling a page of Australian descendants, some of whom now live in Switzerland and Vancouver, I sent this to my Toronto Cousin who then telephoned the Vancouver family. They now plan to meet their hitherto unknown Australian cousins!

Fascinated by the information accruing, I began to write the family history. I received encouragement to persevere after entering one chapter, The Hungry Thirties, in the Stirling Open Writing Competition 1992. It won first prize - and for me a £50 cheque!

To date I have written ten chapters of a projected fourteen-chapter history. Unfortunately I am constantly correcting. Often a chapter's end becomes its beginning. An endless cascade of ever-changing text until diverted by the lure of yet another competition - the Bruce Henderson Memorial Award of the Aberdeen and N E Scotland Family History Society.

Acknowledgements

I take this opportunity to acknowledge my grateful thanks to three people: **George A Dixon**, Archivist, Central Regional Council, who so patiently and pleasantly answered my queries; to **Ronald J MacGregor**, Elgin, a member of our Family History Society, whom I've never met, but who has provided me with titbits of information which I would never have found unaided. And to local historian, **Duncan Wood**, Seatown, Cullen. None of the three are responsible for any errors arising in this book.

George Anderson Clarke

Blairlogie
Stirling

DESKFORD PARISH

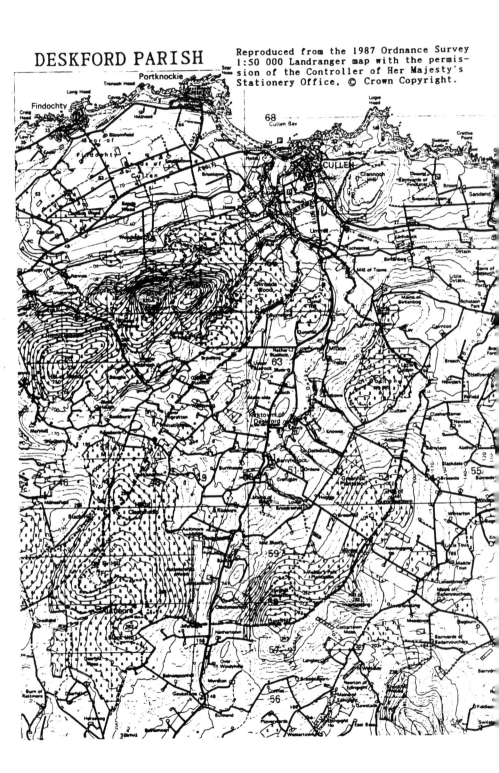

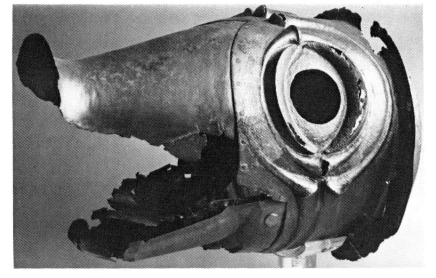

BOAR'S HEAD CARNYX: Proto-Pictish Relic: AD 100-300

1

FROM PICTS TO THE PRESENT

A land of bygone bogs of peat and moss which felt the feet of Roman Legions. A place boasting three pre-Reformation castles with adjoining chapels and from time to time parcelled-out by medieval monarchs. Its Annals mention illicit stills and smugglers, even "pirates" but rarer still and one of only six in Europe's history - a boar's head carnyx. All of that, and much more in a parish called Deskford. Known locally as *Deskert* although the spelling has varied over the centuries from *Deskfurde* to *Deskfoord*, the latter being preferred by the Laird, James(1714-70), Lord Ogilvy, Lord *Deskfoord*, the *Mad Earl* who murdered his Factor and later committed suicide.[1]

Two thousand years ago our Deskford ancestors the Proto-Picts frightened their foes by blowing the carnyx, a long trumpet which emitted a fearsome sound from its "bell" end, a life-size replica of the head of a boar. The boar was a cult animal of the Picts. A boar's head carnyx fashioned from bronze sheets, with a wooden tongue and springs to activate its mouth, was found buried 6ft(2m) deep at Leitchestown farm in 1816. John Anderson, my gt gt Grandfather, handed over this Pictish relic to the Laird's brother, Colonel Francis William Ogilvie-Grant, who had it placed in the Banff Institution.[2]

Deskford, for such a small place, had more than its share of castles: in the *Annals of Cullen, 961-1904*, for 1541 we note:

An old castle or manor of Echinaltry[Inaltry].[3]

Inaltry was farmed in the late eighteenth and early nineteenth centuries by Alex Anderson, who was the brother of John Anderson of Leitchestown(the adjoining farm). Excavations at Inaltry in 1788 uncovered a deep circular chamber thought to be a *dry pit* for holding prisoners, as in medieval castle dungeons. Also, a large metal crucifix was found, which gave rise to the theory that Inaltry meant altar, suggesting ecclesiastical connections. Deskford Tower had a chapel.[2]

Deskford was first mentioned in a Charter dated 27 March 1325 from King Robert the Bruce to a Sir Christian of Forbes, a Knight, where the King conferred on him:

a third part of a davoch [an old land measure] of Ardache [today's Ardoch] and of Skeith [a castle then, thereafter a farm] in the barony of Deskford.[4]

King Robert's second wife, Elizabeth, died on 7 November 1327 in Cullen where he endowed a chaplaincy to her memory,in St Mary's Church.[3]

In 1799 the Rev Walter Chalmers, parish minister, wrote:

The name Deskford derives from *Chessfure*, meaning, a cold place to the southward.[5]

However, his fellow cleric, the Rev William Lawtie, minister of the adjoining parish of Fordyce, suggested *Decius's Fort* meaning a Roman Fort as the origin since Roman coins had been found there.[5] Since another Roman coin, of the Emperor, Claudius Gothicus, AD 268-270, was found at Lintmill in 1890, I tend to favour the Roman Fort theory.[3]

Deskford is one of the smaller parishes on the eastern boundary of Moray District (itself an area steeped in history: famous for Macbeth, its one-time Mormaer and, from 1040-57, Scotland's king). The parish comprises 8,000 acres (3,239 hectares) of fertile farmland stretching for five miles(8 km) astraddle the Keith to Cullen road which, with the Deskford Burn flowing north to the sea at Cullen, roughly bisects its three-mile(5km) width. The parishes of Cullen, Fordyce, Grange and Rathven, encircle the area forming a strath, referred-to locally as the *Howe o' Deskert*. The *Howe* nestles amidst six hills: the Cotton and Summertown in the east, the Lurg and Aultmore in the south, and the Blackhill and the Bin, the highest one of the six at 1,050 ft(330m), in the west.

At the centre of the parish are the church and school on opposite sides of the Keith to Cullen road. In my schooldays I could lean over the playground wall and touch a milestone showing 4 miles(6km) to Cullen and 9 miles(14km) to Keith. In 1992 I looked for it, but in vain. In World War II it was buried to hinder an invading army from knowing their whereabouts. That milestone, behind which I hid my cricket bat, may yet lie interred, never more to see the light of day.

As recently as 1799 the Keith to Cullen highway was the only through-road in the parish. Road maintenance was provided by the local people turning out in spring and autumn, fulfilling a statutory obligation, to patch up potholes, though lacking the benefit of skilled supervision.[5] The Turnpike Act, 1751 allowed the use of Toll Bars to recover maintenance costs. There was a Toll House at each end of the parish on the Keith to Cullen road, and both are occupied as residences in 1992.

In the seventeenth century the only roads would have been muddy tracks across a treeless landscape, broken only by broom, gorse and rushes, with no hedges, dykes or fences separating the fields as today.[6] The Rev George Innes in 1836:

In Deskford, till lately, there has not been one foot of turnpike road.[2]

The first roads to cross the Keith to Cullen highway would have been one from Berryhillock leading east towards Cornhill and another by the School leading west to Rathven and Buckie.

Ownership of land in Deskford, like other parts of Scotland, has changed hands many times, either at the whim of a monarch or through a marriage inheritance. Ancestors of the present owners, the Ogilvie family, inherited control in 1436 when Sir Walter Ogilvy married Margaret Sinclair, daughter of Sir John Sinclair who was killed at the Battle of Harlaw.[3]

Sir Walter Ogilvy was living in Findlater Castle [situated 2 miles(3km) east of Cullen] when, on 9 February 1445:

> he obtained the Royal Licence of King James II for building towers and fortalices in his Castle of Findlater.[3]

In the Annals of Cullen, 961-1904, there is an intriguing entry for the year 1458:

> A declaration by Margaret Ogilvy, Lady Deskford, that she is not detained against her will, in the Castle of Findlater.[3]

It is likely that she was detained, but by whom and why?

Another mystery is recorded for the year 1520:

> King James V confirms a charter of Alexander Ogilvy, by which he granted to Elizabeth Craufurde, for the wrong done to her by him, and for the support of herself and off-spring, for life, the lands of Skeith, in the barony of Deskfurde or Ogilvy.[3]

Medieval Scotland was noted for the savage treatment of its wrong-doers by their being cast into castle dungeons until they died, but even as recently as 1697, we note:

> That George Syme and John Ritchisone, were accused, before the Sheriff, of stealing from the Kilnbarn of Inaltrie, ane load of oats and two panfulls of sowens, which being proven against you have incurred the payne of death...And, in 1699, James Gray, was hanged on Gallows Knowe [a high piece of ground near Clunehill] for stealing a cow. His uncle, in whose barn the cow was killed, was whipped about the gibbet and his ear was nailed thereto, and he was thereafter banished [from] the shire.[3]

Unbelievable barbarity - and less than three centuries ago!

Not all important happenings reach the history books; sometimes they're hushed-up:Lord Deskfoord(1714-70), mentioned earlier, took his own life by slashing his wrists, but newspapers only reported a death, not a suicide. What torments were in his mind? Was it guilt? Four years earlier the death of his Factor, Alexander Grant, had been hushed-up: Lord Deskfoord, in a "mad fit" had stabbed him to death![1]

Grumpy Scot-hater, Dr Samuel Johnson, and his lap-dog Scots companion and biographer, James Boswell, passed through Deskford in 1773 on their tour of Scotland. Little love was lost for the Doctor as we can infer from the Rev Walter Chalmers' chiding words:

> If the famous Dr Johnson in directing his tour through Deskford had deigned to pull down the blinds of his carriage, he would have seen many trees not unworthy of attention even from the most prejudiced English traveller. In an orchard, adjoined to an ancient Castle there is, particularly, an ash tree, measuring in girth, twenty-four feet five and a half inches [8ft thick!]. It is called St John's Tree.[5]

The Doctor apparently did draw up the blinds of his carriage when passing through Cullen where he breakfasted on 28 August, three weeks before his 64th birthday.[3]

Religious relics crop up again; this time in 1890 at Skeith farm where the remains of a Chapel to *Our Lady of Pity* along with her wooden image, were dug up. The date and origin of the Chapel is not clear although there was a Charter dated 1537, recorded in *Stuarts's Records of the Monastery of Kinloss*, whereby lands in Strathislay and Deskford were granted by the Abbot and Convent of Kinloss to Alexander Ogilvy.[7]

Deskford Kirk was involved in the Disruption of 1843: the Rev George Innes, walked out with all of his Kirk Session except one, plus most of his congregation. That's loyalty![7]

An event in my own lifetime concerning two *Deskert loons*, hit the headlines in 1936 when they and two others hijacked a Grimsby-based trawler, the Girl Pat. While being chased across the high seas they hit a sandbank; finally ending-up in Georgetown, Guiana. Both the skipper, Dod Osborne, and the ship's cook, Howard Stephen aged 17, had been brought-up by Deskford foster parents. The other crew members involved were, Dod Osborne's brother as the ship's Mate and, a Harry Stone. The Skipper and Mate served prison terms for the high-jacking, but Howard because of his youth, and Harry Stone, got off.

I was five years younger than *Howie*, as we called him at school. I recall Howie using some of his new-found wealth, from the sale of his story to the News of the World, to put on a fascinating firework display in Berryhillock where he and his sister Joan lived, with Kate Donald. *Howie* on leaving school had worked at Ordens, the farm adjoining ours; later, he and his sister, Joan, joined their father in Grimsby where Joan died at the age of 17. *Howie* now lives in Cornwall.

One of Deskford's best-kept secrets concerns the last war. In the dark days of 1940 when the German army was sweeping across Europe, fears of an invasion arose. However, Deskford's "secret army" was ready, with its underground Nissen bunker with concealed square openings at each end, its bunk beds, seats, table, and a supply of tinned food. In a nearby bunker there was a cache of grenades and Thompson sub-machine guns.[8]

The "army" consisted of a Sergeant (a Deskford farmer who, even today fifty years later prefers anonymity) and eight other specially selected Home Guarders, chosen at the request of a Major Torrance. The nine were sworn to secrecy, not even telling their wives of their role. The operation was taken so seriously that any deserters were to be summarily shot![8]

In the event of an invasion the nine were to hide in the bunker; their task to harass the enemy and report to our own soldiers on enemy troop movements. Thankfully, this army was never tested. Four members are still alive today, in 1992.[8]

As a member of the RAF Cadets, in 1943, I took part in exercises with the Home Guard (*Dad's Army*, they were called) but I never knew of this "army" - a well kept secret indeed![8]

While the preceding is the stuff of history I like to think that real history is about the lives of ordinary people. Let us look at a *loon* growing up with his family, on a Deskford farm, in an age which I have designated *The Hungry Thirties*.

HOGGIE: farmed by Clarkes from 1806 to 1956

2

THE HUNGRY THIRTIES

That I lived to draw my pension is thanks to whisky. Although walking at six months, at age four I was taken ill with pleurisy and, by the doctor's diagnosis, destined to die. In a bold bid to save me Father forced a few drops of whisky past my lips - and it worked! I lived to be told the tale and to learn that whisky is truly the *water of life* - a must for every medicine chest. Being born in a crofter's cottage in Deskford in north-east Scotland on a cold December day in 1924 life was a lottery. Infant deaths were normal then. The first, third and sixth-born of our family of nine all died in infancy. I was the eighth-born of our family.

Six-feet(2m)-deep snowdrifts were not uncommon. In 1947 we were snowed-in to an extent I had not seen before and after digging our way out we walked on top of the snow and actually had to bend down to touch the telephone wires, so deep were the drifts. In winter we kept a shovel behind the door to dig our way to the well across the road.

Occasionally, roads would be blocked for two or three weeks by which time the two shops in Berryhillock village would have run out of groceries. My late Uncle, Jimmy Muiry, a tailor turned grocer with petrol-pump, who owned and had run the shop at the top of the village since 1923, would organise a trip by horse-sledge to Cullen some four miles away for emergency supplies of groceries.

Farm houses in the 1930s did not have central heating nor wall-to-wall carpeting. Our living-room floor comprised 4ft(1.3m) square flagstones of slate some of which acted as a barometer to advise impending rain by exuding damp. The only floor covering was a *clippy-mat* in front of the expansive fireplace with its ingle nooks and huge cast-iron kettle hung high on the sway. The peat fire was hot enough to burn our bare legs tartan while our backs felt like blocks of ice.

One of my Saturday jobs was fetching the messages; it was better than farm-work which I detested (it interfered with my reading!). Newspapers and magazines were read from cover to cover adverts and all. I would have read the proverbial label on the sauce bottle - only we couldn't afford such a luxury!

At Uncle Jimmy's I would buy bread, biscuits, tea, sugar, rice, split-peas, syrup, etc. I wonder if Uncle Jimmy ever knew how I diddled him one day. I was sent for syrup with a shilling(5p) and an empty jar which I handed over for filling-up from the barrel. When Uncle asked for the money I said that I had given him a shilling so he duly handed over the change. Later, spreading my *piece*, there, at the bottom of the jar, was a shiny shilling! Recalling it now I am surprised that my parents did not send me straight back with my ill-gotten gains; they were that kind of people.

Although already laden I would now go to the shop at the foot of the village owned by the Misses Reid sisters, to get paraffin for our *Tilley* - my, that was a major technological advance on the traditional wick lamp, though pumping it up scared the living daylights out of us in case it exploded! I would also buy a few candles, a large box of matches and an ounce of *Bogie Roll* tobacco for Father. This was cut from an uncoiled one pound roll which was measured along a brass ruler set into the counter. For Mother I got two ounces of cloves. The only time I was persuaded to try one was to cure my toothache, but it didn't. Occasionally, a rare treat, a quarter-pound of pandrops.

I wonder why I was never tempted to pinch a pandrop on the mile-long trudge home? Maybe the explanation lies in the example set by our Parents; for instance, money would lie in a bowl on the sideboard, yet we were never tempted to help our-selves to a penny; it would have been a violation of the trust which our Parents placed in us.

On returning from RAF service in India in 1947 I recall Mother telling me about the orphan boy whom she had taken in during the war. Ten-year-old Tommy regularly helped himself to the loose change. Such breach of trust simply broke Mother's heart - he had to go. In fairness, I suppose the instillation of integrity and trust begin at an early age. Don't the Jesuits say, "Give us a child until the age of seven"?

I hated farm work, but one job I liked was helping my Father cast peats during the school holidays at the Moss in Grange, some six miles away. We would cycle there, complete with bottles of cold tea and milk which we buried in the wet moss to keep them cool. We did not have thermos flasks then. Our *piece* was bread and cheese and home-baked scones.

Father cut the peats and I laid them on the heather to dry until sufficiently hard to stack in fours. Twenty score was needed to tide us over the winter. After a couple of good drying days we would gather them ready for carting home. I felt sorry for our twenty-year-old horse, Star, having to pull the heavy box-cart with its iron-rimmed wheels. In the stable, Star needed a strong leather band slung behind his stall to sit back on to sleep, since, if he lay down a block and tackle was needed to get him on his feet again. Poor Star!

Near the Moss were roofless ruins of derelict houses. Questioning Father about this I got a brief history lesson:

The families emigrated to survive, because no work was available then, or now.

I have never forgotten the hint of anger in Father's voice. In retrospect I suppose my political beliefs began to form then.

At the edge of the Moss in the only remaining thatched cottage next door to the then derelict Poor's House, lived Granny Christie aged 80 in 1932. Granny Christie had four children, yet she never married. Half a century later, when checking the 1891 Census I saw listed Isabella Christie aged 38 and three of her four children, the youngest aged three, being my Mother, Sarah Ann McNamara Christie. Also recorded, was Granny's Mother, Margaret Christie (nee Reaper) aged 76, described as pauper. No Social Security hand-outs in those days - only the ignominy of being branded a pauper because you were on Parish Relief! No wonder Mother used to put the frighteners on us whenever we lavished syrup on our piece, by saying, "You'll have us all in the Poor's House!"

To dodge the dreaded farm work I would disappear to the Deskford Burn with my wannie and girn. I would wait patiently by the deep pools for a trout to appear, then stealthily manoeuvre the girn over its gills and with a deft flip of my wannie, I would land my trout. In the shallows I would guddle for trout lurking under stones. I have seen me go home with up to ten trout, from six to nine inches long. I would gut them, sprinkle them with oatmeal, fry them in butter, then scoff the lot the same night. Sixty years later I am still slavering at the remembered aroma and taste. I am also reminded of the fishy taste of sea-gull's eggs which we gathered from the nearby Lurg Hill, in early May. Another remembered taste and smell is, of eating a penny poke of chips at Peter Fair. Also known as Rathven Market this fair was held on the third Friday of July,it originated over three hundred years ago in 1686, as a horse fair. The name, Peter, derives from St Peter's Church which in 1226 was granted money "to set up a leper house for seven persons." Around the 1800s the fair was also a feeing market for farm servants.[1]

In the 1930s most of the sideshows at the fair were cons; i.e. you were inveigled to part with your money by a slick patter promising daring revelations! There were boxing booths where one could earn a fiver by holding-out for three rounds against a professional boxer. It was a sad sight to see Gorbals-born Benny Lynch (1913-46), former Scottish fly-weight champion, reduced to earning a living by bruising with farm hands - and drinking himself to death at the early age of 33!

I remember the thrilling, but dreaded, *Wall of Death* where a pair of motor cyclists rode round at high speed in opposite directions on the inside wall of a circular building. We viewed this dangerous spectacle from an upper platform around the top of the wall. There were roundabouts, *chair-o-planes*, fortune tellers and roll-a-penny stalls enclosed with wire-netting to prevent punters surreptitiously re-positioning their penny onto a winning square. I can still hear the stall-holder shouting incessantly, "In the square we pay your fare; on the line the money's mine." Most of the five *bob* (25p) I had saved-up from my Saturday pennies landed on the lines.

My Father, John Clarke, was better known as "Johnny Hoggie". In reply to the auctioneer's "Sold to?", he would reply, "Clarke, Hoggie" and so the farm name stuck, as a surname. Once I stayed away from school to help my Father drive stirks to Cornhill Mart some five miles away, only to trudge back home with them unsold, due, as Father said, to dealers rigging the market. Such setbacks never seemed to bother Father, but reflecting on it now I wonder how he felt arriving home without any money. Young as I was I felt like cursing. Only once did I hear my Father swear. A man called-in one day to buy some straw, but offered such an insultingly low price that Father retorted, "Go to Hell!" To me that was swearing.

Mother, in contrast, was less calm. I recall her once, seething with anger when offered only sixpence (2.5p) for one dozen eggs from the grocer who called weekly. "We'll eat them and the hens as well before selling at that price!" We did just that; eggs galore and chickens too; like fighting cocks we lived. But, Oh! how I longed for the taste of butcher meat.

Of course, Jim Garden, the grocer's salesman, was only doing his boss's bidding. Jim's life was no picnic. I remember him leaving our house at ten which meant he wouldn't get to Keith till after midnight, and before turning-in for the night he would have to feed and water his horse. Next day Jim would be up before six to load up. Asking him once, how he managed with so little sleep, he confided that he was able to get a couple of hours sleep on the way home - his horse knew the way!

Farm servants fared worse. A school-leaver would be paid £10 or less, not per week or month, but at the end of the six-month hiring, in May and November! Unmarried men slept in the *chaumer* and got their meals in the farmhouse kitchen. Breakfast, in the words of the old bothy ballad, *The Hash of Drumdelgie*, would "Generally be brose". In 1934 I spent a holiday at Drumdelgie, where my Brother-in-law was a ploughman. He told me once how a young lad had dared to ask the farmer for a sub, i.e. an advance on his pay, only to be brusquely reminded that, "You get free milk, free meal and free tatties - what more do you want?" To this the lad meekly replied,"I need to buy some salt".

Threshing day was the only day of the year when I liked farm work. Dod Anderson, a Cousin from Portsoy, owned a "stem mull", our name for a threshing mill. *Aul 'Dod* was tall with black tousled hair and face to match, ingrained from years of smoke; his pristine "ivories" shone as he flashed a smile, or cursed a mill-feeder for letting an unfastened sheaf into the mill, choking it and making the engine "belch". *Aul'Dod* could tell what was happening to the mill by the variation in sound.

I was fascinated by this hissing, belching monster with its two madly-rotating balls above the boiler. Then, I could only guess their purpose, but learnt during my RAF training as a flight-engineer that the centrifugal force of the spinning balls actuated a valve to govern the engine speed.

It was an education to watch *Aul' Dod* manoeuvring this monster, frantically rotating the shiny steering wheel, yet moving the front wheels only an inch or two (no sophisticated power-steering, then!). Or to observe that endearing habit of doffing his smoke-stained cap whilst scratching his *pow*, as if pondering a problem; a kind of nervous twitch, I think.

On threshing day, neighbours helped, since it needed at least ten men to tend the mill: two to pitch the sheaves on to the mill, two to feed them into the shredder, three to build the *soo* of straw as it tumbled from the conveyor belt, two to sack-up the corn and carry it to the loft, and one other, usually me, to clear the chaff. Sometimes I would desert my post to help a terrier chase a rat dislodged from its cosy home in the ricks, only to scurry back mighty fast on hearing the curses of the men moving the corn as they got their feet entangled in a growing pile of chaff.

For Mother, threshing day was all go since she had to feed the *brutes*. Mother would fill the big pot with *intilts* to produce a broth so thick that you could stand up a spoon in it. Any left-overs would be re-heated to feed the family. Where did all the salmonella and listeria bugs we now hear so much about, lurk, in those days? Also, hopefully there might be some scones and bannocks as leftovers. To seat everyone the dining table was extended by boards on trestles and covered with freshly laundered bed sheets as tablecloths.

Our grain loft was riddled with rats. On the promise of being paid a penny a pair I set out to make a fortune with my *multi-killing-machine*. This was a barn door propped-up with a V-shaped stick to which was attached a length of binder-twine, sufficiently long to reach under the loft door where I kept watch. Whilst the rats busily munched the bruised-corn bait, I pulled the string to release the heavy door on top of them. I soon learnt about the "law of diminishing returns"; I worked myself out of a job - I should have left some rats to breed!

Another earner was catching moles. Brother John paid me a penny for every mole-skin I provided which he then sold at an inflated profit. I did the hard graft of trapping, skinning and drying the mole-skins, but ended up being paid a pittance - while the *Boss* got the cream. Exploitation even between brothers! The tale of Brother John's other entrepreneurial enterprises has still to be told.

Before Wireless our only entertainment was to invite Harry Tamson, a local farm worker, with his gramophone. Harry often invited himself: one Saturday he turned up uninvited at sister Madge's, stayed overnight but never offered to pay a penny; not that Madge would have taken anything. A night with Harry started about eight and ended next morning about three, a non-stop cabaret of Scottish music interspersed with gossip, jokes and many cups of tea. These were nights of laughter, long remembered. The last I heard of Harry was when a pulley flew off a machine and broke his jaw, but I am sure that would not have suppressed him. Harry was a legend in his own life-time; but he was a victim of the march of technology - the Wireless. Brother John began to dabble in radio and soon he was supplying households throughout the parish with plastic-cased radio sets. The gramophone's era was o'er!

When I first went to school, in 1929, the infants' class had to make do with slates on which to write. The slate pencil, a *scailie*, sometimes would screech unbearably. My slate, in its wooden frame, measured about 10 x 7 inches (25 x 18cm). We were supposed to clean our slate by wiping it with a wet rag but more often than not we chose the quicker, more unhygienic, method of spitting on it and wiping it dry with our sleeve!

Being Dux of Deskford School, at age thirteen, was a major factor in saving me from becoming a farm servant. I was persuaded by the Headmaster, John A Beveridge, or *JAB*, as we called him, to continue my studies at Buckie High School. *JAB* was an unusual Headmaster, introducing many novel ideas. For example, boys from age twelve underwent a year of domestic science along with the girls, for whom it was compulsory.

Another innovation, was to give us newspapers to read and then quiz us about their political slants; thus we learnt about the hidden power of the *press barons*. We also did the crosswords and compiled our own, which helped immensely to expand our vocabulary. When teaching us geometry, *JAB* gave us a surveyor's tape and told us to draw-up a plan of the school; an enjoyable way of learning. Our school was built in 1876, four years after the 1872 Education Act which inaugurated compulsory State education. When my Father started school in 1876, instead of going to the former Church school, he went to a brand new public school, the one I was now measuring-up some sixty years later.

Another *JAB* novelty was taking the whole class to his house on Monday 1 June 1936 to listen to a radio programme about the *Queen Mary*, setting off on her maiden voyage two-years after her launch. That was real teaching. *JAB* also told us that, by wide reading and travelling, schooling would be unnecessary. To our parents, steeped in the tradition of "teaching by the tawse" that was heresy. *JAB* was a Dominie ahead of his time.

In 1936, I, along with four other boys, by-passed a class because *JAB* believed us capable of coping with a higher level. This inflated our egos but in retrospect I have mixed feelings about such segregation since it creates tensions between the chosen few and those left to hang as they grow! I now believe that too much attention is paid to clever ones, and too little to plodders. My feelings on this, are best illustrated by the story of the little boy comparing his small helping with the larger helping on his older brother's plate: on complaining to his mother about such injustice, she pointed out to him that he was only a little boy, to which he retorted, "I'll always be a little boy if I get small helpings!"

School dinners were non-existent in the *Thirties*. In winter we got cocoa, served-up in wide-brimmed enamel bowls which, judging by their chipped state, might well have been throw-outs from a Poor House! When filled, you could hardly hold the bowl let alone allow it near your lips. Yet, in two minutes flat your cocoa was ice-cold. We ate our piece standing up. Mine was less than appetising, being two *doorsteps*, spread with *Lyle's Golden Syrup* which had soaked into the bread, to be washed down with cocoa, cold as charity! One time we had an endless supply of syrup; Mother bought a two-gallon(9 litre) pailful. By the time we got to the last two inches it had crystallised. We pinched a spoonful of that occasionally!

My thirst for reading was sated by having to choose books from the Mobile County Library for a neighbouring farmer, William Currie. Willie was a Liberal County Councillor; he and my Mother, who was then a Tory, had ding-dong political arguments. My bent for politics began to form at this time.

I would scan the library books before handing them over. One which I read non-stop was called *Kaput*, by Carveth Wells, about his travels in Russia after the Revolution of 1917. Carveth was an anti-Communist, his main theme being that nothing in Russia worked, that everything was *Kaput*, a German word meaning broken. The word *Kaput* cropped-up on nearly every page. The travelogue fascinated me. Strangely enough, the only other book which I ever read through non-stop, was George Orwell's *Animal Farm*, whose theme was also anti-Communism.

Other sources of reading for me were women's magazines like *The People's Friend* and *Red Letter*. I remember Annie S Swan as a fascinating writer. I can still recall the Red Barn Murder Mystery and other thrillers in the *Red Letter*. These weeklies were bought by the Murrays of Hollanbush, our nearest neighbour with whom we exchanged the *People's Journal* and the *Banffshire Journal (Banffy)* - another of my Saturday jobs.

I also raided the bookcase which Brother John had bought at an auction.There I found Jack London's *Iron Heel* which covered the struggles of the American working class and, *The Ragged Trousered Philanthropists*, written in 1909 by Robert Tressell, a Hastings house painter, about the struggles which he and his fellow workers had to get decent wages. Before that bookcase arrived the only books which we had were the Bible - (obligatory then, even if only to record the family births) and *Be Your Own Family Doctor*, equally vital living, as we did, four miles from the nearest doctor and before the advent of the National Health Service. Because of the illustrations we were forbidden to look at this book - but we did!

Attending High School meant ten miles of arduous biking over the Bin Hill, 1,050ft(330m) high, to Buckie, unlike the 1990s when a taxi would have been provided. In winter I cycled to Tochieneal station to get the train; but I felt guilty about the added cost as I was sure my parents could ill afford it.

Buckie High School was run on the Comprehensive principle: An *A* stream for those following an Academic course; *B* for Commercial studies; and *C* for Technical. I chose the *C* stream.

One major difference in this school was that we changed teachers and class rooms every forty minutes, unless we happened to have a double period. This moving was terribly time-wasting; the teachers should have moved, not us! While at science lessons, I was surprised to see, in an adjoining room, fishermen studying for Captain's and Mate's certificates.

I was at Buckie High School on Friday 1 September 1939 when our Art teacher, Geordie Coutts, told us that he had just heard that Hitler was about to invade Poland. As we talked, Mr Coutts's daughter Isobel came into the room and asked her father what was happening; when told that war with Germany was imminent, her response is still memorable: "Oh, is that all!"

Biking to Buckie High school I went past a farm called Mains of Buckie little realising until recently, some fifty years later, that my gt gt gt Grandparents, James Clarke and Elspet Andrew, had farmed there from 1751 until 1771. At Whitsun 1771 they moved to Raemore and began nearly two centuries of Clarke descendants, farming in three separate Deskford farms and associated with a fourth farm when my Grandfather, James Clarke, married Ann Anderson, the daughter of another long established Deskford farmer, John Anderson, of Leitchestown.[2]

THE CLARKES & RELATED FAMILIES IN FOUR DESKFORD FARMS

YEAR	RAEMORE	MID SKEITH	HOGGIE	LEITCHESTOWN
1771	James Clarke* Elspet Andrew	TENANTED	TENANTED	TENANTED
1785				Alex Anderson Mgt.Steinson
1795		Alex Clarke (son of JC/EA) Isbl.Shepherd		
1804				John Anderson Ann Wright
1806			James Clarke Lilias Hood	
1812	NEW TENANT			
1832		Alex Clarke & son James		
1837			John Clarke son of JC/LH	
1848		James Clarke Mgt.Mitchell		
1851				Heirs of John Anderson
1863				Jms. Anderson Brbra.Russell
1879				NEW TENANT
1883	Jas.Maitland Isbla.Clarke	James Clarke Ann Anderson		
1896			Elspet(Eppy) Clarke Illegitimate dau.of Jn.C & Mgt.Sinclair	
1903		Ann Anderson & son John		
1910	Jas.Maitland Sen(1838-1914) Jun(1865-1943)	Ann Anderson & son Alex	John Clarke Sarah Mackie	
1913		Alex Clarke (1874-1957)		
1933	NEW TENANT			
1943		NEW TENANT		
1954			Sarah Clarke	
1956			NEW TENANT	

* **JC & EA at Mains of Buckie, Rathven from 1751 - 1771**
Note:Tenanted/New Tenant implies not related to Clarkes

12

MID SKEITH: farmed by Clarkes from 1795 to 1943

3

INHERITANCE LOST

Illness and infant deaths were commonplace before the creation of the National Health Service in 1948. I quote the first page of a letter written by my Father (then aged 13) to his Uncle, Captain John Clarke (1847-97), Quebec Province, Canada on a frosty Saturday 21 February 1885 (severe frost had held-up ploughing for over three weeks, according to Father's letter):

> Dear Uncle,
>
> we received your letter stating your bad health but I hope you are getting better. We have had a lot of dis-health here for the past three weeks. Baby and your Mother both grew ill on the same day. Baby lived a week, she died on 7 February, aged six months. It was inflammation of the lungs that was the matter with both of them. Your Mother is still in bed. My Father was very ill with pleurisy on the lungs. He has been in bed for the past fortnight but he is getting the length of the fireside, now, but very weak.

With the death of his baby sister of six months a fortnight earlier, his Father and Grandmother both ill and his Uncle John's ill health, it must have seemed a most depressing world for a thirteen-year-old growing up at Mid Skeith in 1885.

My gt gt gt Grandparents, James Clarke and Elspet Andrew married in 1751. They farmed Mains of Buckie, Rathven, for twenty years, until Whitsun 1771, after which they came to Deskford to take over the tenancy of Raemore.[1]

In 1795, Alexander (1765-1850), second eldest son of James and Elspet, took on the tenancy of Mid Skeith, one of the largest farms in Deskford, at 111 acres(45 hectares),just over half a mile(1km) away across the valley from Raemore.[2] In 1800 Alexander married Isobel Shepherd (1780-1850); they had four sons and three daughters. Their youngest, John (1819-66), graduated M.A. at Kings College, Aberdeen in 1842; after eleven years teaching he became Minister of Knockando Church.[3]

Gt gt Grandfather Alexander (1765-1850) was a meticulous keeper of records: I have a copy of a Seafield Estates receipt dated 2 August 1799, for £25 annual rent paid. Alexander, at the age of sixty-seven, made his eldest son James (1801-84) joint tenant, ready to inherit on his death; he died in 1850.

In 1839, gt Grandfather James married Margaret Mitchell (1814-85); they had five sons and four daughters; the last three died young: George died in July 1856 after only two weeks of life; Ann, aged 7 and Jane, aged 10, both died during the weekend of 25/26 February 1865 of diphtheria, after two weeks illness. James(1845-1903), the eldest son, took over the tenancy on the death of his father in 1884.

In 1869, Grandfather James married Ann Anderson (1846-1913) from Leitchestown, another big farm, some three miles (5km) away which had been farmed by her ancestors since 1785. James and Ann had three sons and four daughters. The sixth-born, Jessie Anderson, died at the age of six months in 1885. My Father, John, was the second-born of the family in 1871.

Uncle James (1870-1969), eldest son, and heir to the tenancy of Mid Skeith, left home at age 19 and became a dress salesman in Glasgow. Why did he leave and forego his inheritance? Was he fed up living in a rather dilapidated house? Actually, Mid Skeith was completely re-built the following year, in 1890. Maybe, like me, he did not fancy farm work. Too late to ask him now; he died in 1969, five months short of his centenary. Uncle James married Elizabeth (Bessie) Waddell in 1898 in Glasgow; they named their house, Deskford. Uncle became joint owner of a high-class furrier's business in prestigious Sauchiehall Street; he had a keen business sense, keeping up-to-date by making flying visits to Paris to view the latest fashions. However, I remember Uncle James for his very welcome, annual, family-size Xmas box of Birrels chocolates.

When Grandfather James died in 1903 his widow, Ann, made her second son, John (my Father) joint tenant, in readiness to take over on her death. Four years later my Father, aged 35, married Sarah Ann McNamara Mackie, aged 19. Now, with such a name, you would expect a lengthy family pedigree; not so, since Sarah's Mother, Isabella Christie (1852-1945) never married, although she had four children - to four different fathers! Sarah, (reputed father, William Mackie) the youngest of the four children, was born in 1888. Flouting the conventions of the 1880s took exceptional courage. Others, less charitable, would probably label her a brazen hussy!

I spent a holiday with Granny Christie in 1932 when I was eight and she eighty. Granny's place, Hillhead of Kilbady in Grange, was an ancient clay-built, earthen-floored, thatched but-and-ben, with a wooden chimney, which was known as a *hingin'-lum*. Granny's mother had also been born in this two-roomed cottage, so you can imagine its age.

After returning home from holiday I mentioned that I had slept in the bunk-bed with Granny. Mother reached for the *People's Friend* and read me a story about a teacher remonstrating with one of his pupils for being late again. The boy's plaintive and tearful excuse exactly echoed my own sentiments - "I canna climb ower my Granny!" It was an onerous responsibility for an octogenarian to look after an energetic eight year old in such isolation at the edge of the Moss.

Near Granny's cottage were roofless ruins of houses left to rot by families driven to the towns and its alien way of life in search of work - sometimes to emigrate. I remember visiting the home of a retired schoolmaster, James Mair, and witnessing a veritable *Aladdin's Cave,* a room where the walls from floor to ceiling were lined with books. What happened to them?

Searching through the 1891 Grange Census, I noted that Hillhead of Kilbady housed Margaret Christie (nee Reaper,1814-1909) aged 76(head of the household), her daughter Isabella, (my Granny) aged 38; three Grandchildren, Jeannie McGrigor aged 19, Alex A. Smith aged 10 and Sarah Ann McNamara Christie aged 3 (my Mother). Granny's occupation was given as "domestic servant", her mother was listed as - "pauper"! The eldest Granddaughter, Madge, was not included, presumably she was a domestic servant elsewhere. Later, Madge went off to work in the textile mills of northern England, where she married a Jack Hargreaves. For years, some members of our family believed that the Jack Hargreaves who did a TV series called *Out of Town,* **must** be Madge's son. Eventually, in order to put the record straight, I wrote to Jack - we were wrong!

Mother was a milliner in Glasgow before marrying. I think she was proud of having had such a job instead of being a domestic servant, the fate of most young girls in those days. However, having become a farmer's wife she was now tied-down to milking cows, feeding pigs and hens, collecting eggs, making butter and cheese, and a thousand other jobs, leaving no time for fanciful pursuits like millinery.

Compare the background of the Clarkes of Mid Skeith with that of Sarah Ann McNamara Christie (reputed father, William Mackie) of Hillhead of Kilbady: At Mid Skeith, Matriarch Ann, whose forbears had long been Kirk Elders, with sons, John (my Father), *Sandy* (my Uncle), three adult daughters, Maggie Ann, Jeannie, and Jessie Anderson(my Aunts). And into this houshold came young Sarah, a sinner, according to the Kirk! Apart from the difference in social background, there were now five women in one kitchen, truly a recipe for disaster. Family squabbles ensued, ending-up with Grandmother Ann writing her Will on 5 January 1910, helped by the Rev George Mathieson Park, B.D.[4]

The Will clearly demonstrated a household divided: half of the disposable assets was to be divided equally among the whole family of six, but the household contents to be divided only among Sandy, Maggie and Jeannie (Jessie had married and left home in 1908). Uncle Sandy was to receive the other half of the disposable assets and to assume the farm tenancy on his Mother's death. My Parents, feeling snubbed, walked out and Mother never, ever again, crossed the threshold of Mid Skeith. Fortuitously, Hoggie, one mile(1.6km) away, became vacant.[2]

Hoggie, a 21-acre(9 hectare) croft, one-fifth the size of Mid Skeith, first came into Clarke hands in 1806. The tenancy was taken over by my gt gt Granduncle James, elder brother of Alexander who had taken over Mid Skeith in 1795. When my gt gt Granduncle died in 1837, aged 85, his son John, born in 1812, took over the tenancy until his death in 1896 when the tenancy passed to his illegitimate daughter, Elspeth (*Eppy*), jointly with **her** illegitimate son, James Sutherland. *Eppy*, Father's second Cousin, died in 1909, leaving Hoggie vacant till it became a refuge for my parents who moved-in at Whitsun, 1910.[2]

Mother once told us an amusing story about Cousin *Eppy* who, visiting Cullen one day was seen in the middle of Seafield Street, shouting "Help! Help!" Onlookers thought she had "lost her marbles", but she had lost her dog, whose name was "Help."

Imagine the contrast: Mid Skeith, completely rebuilt in 1890 with its modern buildings, an indoor lavatory, bathroom, and water on tap, with Hoggie, a drab dwelling-house with a grain-loft on the upper storey and a haven for rats. With the farm buildings adjoined to the dwelling house it didn't make it any more desirable. At one end was an extension with two bedrooms, above which was a rather draughty garret where three or four of the family slept. Whilst reading or doing my homework the guttering candle sometimes blew-out. On other occasions I have awoken to find a fine layer of snow blown under the eaves at the edge of my chaff-filled palliase.

Our water supply was a well across the road. In winter we often had to dig our way to get to it. To us children this was just ordinary, all that we ever knew, but to our Parents it must have been a galling come-down. Hardly a picnic for Mother - even if she was the only woman in her own kitchen!

Nine were born into our Family but only six survived. The first two, both named John, were born at Mid Skeith: the first in 1908, but dying a month later. The second in 1910 and now in his 83rd year. Next came James in 1911 but he died three months later. Then Madge in 1912, Ernest in 1915, William in 1916 (but died in 1918), Allan in 1920, George (author) 1924 and Leslie, 1930. All six are alive in 1992.

Even in 1910 there was only a bare existence to be had on such a small farm. I cannot recall when Father bought a new suit; but I do remember Brother Ernest writing home in 1938 from a farm in Jersey, telling us about his employer, a farmer, who was also hard-up. His best suit was twenty years old and his Sunday shoes, ten! Ernest's letter came on the same day that Father, cycling home from Keith, found that one side of his jacket was burnt, completely ruining his best suit. Father had carelessly pocketed his pipe while it was still smouldering. Mother was angry, almost in tears - what could Father wear now? This was his one and only suit! People today with their well-stocked wardrobes cannot contemplate how we felt. Even today, sixty years later, an anger wells-up within me as I recall the indignity of that level of poverty.

How different would our lives have been had our Father inherited the tenancy of the 111 acre (45 hectare) Mid Skeith in 1913 and not had to scrimp and scrape for forty-four years in 21 acre (9 hectare) Hoggie? Obviously, our lives would have been easier. What about our education and jobs? Would I have gone to University? Would John have become a miller, or Ernest left home to work for Wimpey, Civil Engineers, or Madge ended-up a farmer, Allan a shepherd, or Leslie a farm grieve?

The history of the people of rural parishes in Scotland in earlier days is very much linked with the Lairds, whose estate management policies could enrich or impoverish their tenants' lives. Of equal importance was the Kirk, whose minister and Elders sought to safeguard their parishioners' morals, and the Dominies, who set even higher standards for their students.

Let us look at each in turn to see if we can establish what effect they had on us and other Deskford families.

TOWER OF DESKFORD: 16th c. Laird's Residence in Kirkton
© Charles McKean, B.A.,F.R.S.A.,F.S.A.(Scot), Hon.F.R.I.B.A.

4

THE LAIRDS

In the fourteenth century the Sinclair family held land and property rights to Deskford, although from 1390 to 1406 the barony of Deskford was in the hands of John, Earl of Moray, brother of King Robert III. In 1411 Sir John Sinclair of Deskford and Findlater was killed at the Battle of Harlaw. Between 1411 and 1435, Sir John's grandson, John, held title to Deskford and was created Lord Deskford in 1420. In 1435, Lord Deskford's heir, Alexander Sinclair, renounced his claim in favour of his aunt, Margaret Sinclair, daughter of the late Sir John. A year later she married Sir Walter Ogilvy of Auchleven. A charter dated 1440 transferred the barony of Deskford and Findlater to Sir Walter Ogilvy and his spouse.[1]

A century later, in 1541, a charter from King James V:

> Confirmed to Alexander Ogilvy and his spouse, Elizabeth Gordon, the lands and barony of Deskford with the Tower and fortalice thereof and the patronage of the Chapel of Deskford.[2]

The Tower was the majestic 4-storey Tower of Deskford, in Kirkton village. Sir John Sinclair would have lived there.

In 1545, Alexander Ogilvy bequeathed everything to his son-in-law, Sir John Gordon, third son of George Gordon, the 4th Earl of Huntly, thereby disinheriting his own son, and in so doing started a feud between the Gordon and Ogilvy families. On 25 June 1562, Sir John Gordon of Deskford, in an argument on the streets of Edinburgh attacked James, Lord Ogilvy.[2]

Queen Mary, recently returned from France, was not amused and ordered the 4th Earl of Huntly to hand over the Castles of Findlater and Auchindoun, which he failed to do. On 28 October, at the Battle of Corrichie, the Earl of Huntly was killed and his son, Sir John Gordon, was taken prisoner and executed as a traitor in Aberdeen. His estates were forfeited and the baronies of Deskford and Findlater were restored to Lord Ogilvy who died in 1574 and was succeeded by his grandson, Sir Walter Ogilvy, Lord Deskford, from 1616.[2]

Around about 1600 Sir Walter Ogilvy of Deskford and Findlater was living in Findlater Castle which was situated about two miles (3km) east of Cullen. This castle was built in 1445, on an exposed promontory, 200 feet above the sea which almost encircled it, like a moat. On the 20 March 1600 Sir Walter gave instructions to dig the founds of a new and grander residence within the environs of Cullen, that is, the Old *Toun* of Cullen. The chosen location, on a rock some fifty feet above the Deskford Burn, was believed to have been the site of an ecclesiastical building some centuries earlier. Sir Walter and his Lady, Dame Mary Douglas (Lady Deskford from 1616), moved into their new home around 1602. The family gallery in the adjoining church bears the date 1602 and the arms and monograms of both Sir Walter and Dame Mary Douglas. Sir Walter died in 1623 and his son, James, inherited the title, Lord Deskford. On 20 February 1638, Lord Deskford was created 1st Earl of Findlater.[2]

In March 1645, Cullen House and the town of Cullen were plundered by the Farquharsons of Braemar, on the orders of the Marquis of Montrose,then fighting against the Covenanters. Lord Ogilvy, 1st Earl of Findlater, was a supporter of the Covenant. Cullen House was only saved from arson on payment of a ransom by Lady Findlater (her husband was in Edinburgh at the time), of 20,000 merks,[£13,000, Scots, £1,125 sterling]. Two months later, Montrose's men returned and burnt-down the whole of Cullen, leaving Cullen House unscathed.[2]

James, Lord Deskford and 1st Earl of Findlater, although twice married, had no male heir, so, in 1641, he procured a new grant of his honours patent which allowed his son-in-law, Sir Patrick Ogilvy of Inchmartine(who had married the Earl's daughter and heiress, Elizabeth) to succeed him. Sir Patrick became 2nd Earl of Findlater in 1652; he died in 1659 and his eldest son, James, inherited the title of 3rd Earl. In turn, James' eldest son, Walter, became Lord Deskford and normally would have inherited the title of 4th Earl, but he died,"before June 1696", ahead of his father. In 1711, James's second son, James (1664-1730), became 4th Earl of Findlater.[1]

James (1664-1730), both before and after inheriting the title of 4th Earl of Findlater, was probably the most active, politically, of the Ogilvy family: Advocate in 1685; M.P. for Cullen, 1689-95; Solicitor General, 1693; Secretary of State, 1695-6 and President of the Scots Parliament. In 1698, as a reward for his political activities, he was created Viscount Seafield and Lord Ogilvy of Cullen. In 1701 he was elevated to 1st Earl of Seafield, Viscount Reidhaven, and Lord Ogilvy of Deskford and Cullen. James also held the following positions:Lord High Chancellor of Scotland, 1702-4 and 1705-7; Lord Chief Baron, 1707; Keeper of the Great Seal, 1713; and Representative Peer, 1707-10, 1712-15, and 1727-30.[2]

James (1664-1730), as Lord Chancellor (1702-7), had led discussions between representatives of the Scottish and English Parliaments on how to bring about a Union of the two Parliaments. In 1707, after signing the Act of Union, Lord Ogilvy uttered the now famous words:

There's ane end of ane auld sang.[3]

The new British Government discriminated against Scotland in its taxation policies: English coal entered Ireland duty-free, Scottish coal could not. England's main export, wool, had a low tax compared with Scotland's linen. In 1712, a tax on salt exports was imposed, adversely affecting fish-curing in villages along the Banffshire coast. Also, in 1713, a malt tax was imposed, which led to riots in 1725. All of these taxes were in violation of the Treaty of Union. When Scotland's M.Ps. complained they were told that Scotland must now put up with English laws! The Earl's support for Union turned sour. In 1713 in the House of Lords he proposed the Dissolution of the Union. He lost, but only by four votes: 67 to 71.[3]

In the 1715 Jacobite Rising, the Earl was imprisoned as being suspected of having Jacobite leanings, i.e. supporting the (Catholic) King James VII, who was deposed in 1689 and replaced by the (Protestant) William and Mary of Orange. The 4th Earl died on 15 August 1730 and was succeeded by his son, James, as 5th Earl of Findlater and 2nd Earl of Seafield. James became Vice Admiral of Scotland.[2]

Cullen House was then ransacked for the second time in a century! On 9 April 1746 (a week before the Culloden massacre) Bonnie Prince Charlie's Highlanders, pursued by the Duke of Cumberland's soldiers, plundered the House. The 5th/2nd Earl escaped, although his Factor, Alexander Grant, was imprisoned in his own house at nearby Tochieneal farm. The cost of the destruction was estimated at £8,000 sterling.[2]

James Ogilvy, 5th Earl of Findlater and 2nd of Seafield, died in 1764 and was succeeded by his son, James (1714-70).[2]

James (1714-70), before inheriting the titles in 1764 of 6th Earl of Findlater, 3rd Earl of Seafield, and Lord Deskfoord, had made a name for himself, not as a politician like his father and grandfather, but as an agricultural improver. In 1748 the Earl encouraged investors to finance the manufacture of linen and damask in Cullen and to set up a lint mill, nearby, hence the name of the village there, now - Lintmill. Four years later another entrepreneur started a Bleachfield in Deskford. By 1799, according to the Rev Walter Chalmers:

> There are whitened yearly about 1500 pieces of cloth and 1700 spindles of thread and yarn.[4]

However, by 1836, the Rev George Innes was writing:

> From the falling off of the linen trade in this quarter, it has turned out, latterly, quite a losing concern and has been given up; the machinerey remaining a dead stock on the owner's hand and the Bleachfield being converted into corn-land.[5]

Lord Deskfoord sought to make improvments in agriculture by encouraging his tenants to send their sons to English farms to study their methods. Also, he introduced a system of crop rotation which Lord (Turnip) Townshend (1674-1738) had started in England some years earlier. Rotating root, grain and grass crops in the same field, it was discovered, rested the soil, reduced weeds and increased yields. Turnips were introduced into Deskford by Lord Deskfoord. Farmers today no longer need to follow the 7-year crop rotation system because of improved fertilisers and weed killers; but this has brought its own problems. Consumers today, in the 1990s, are demanding vegetables cultivated organically with natural fertilisers.

By 1752, Lord *Deskfoord* had arranged the planting of 32 million trees. An innovation to protect them from theft was to confer, on some tenants, an entitlement at their lease-end, to every third tree or its value in money. The 7th Earl of Seafield, John Charles Ogilvie-Grant, between 1853 and 1881, arranged the planting of 60 million more trees. Wood was invaluable to the Seafield Estates for building work, fencing and firewood, as well as sales to timber merchants.[2]

The Rev Walter Chalmers, in 1799, wrote:

> The Common pasture known as Green Hill, on the east side of the vale was enclosed and divided with dike and hedge, belts of Scotch fir and alder planted and a complete set of farm houses built, but after considerable expense his Lordship was discouraged; the enclosures are now let annually, for pasture. On the west side, on a hill called Old More, the late Lord Findlater [committed suicide in 1770] parcelled out the skirts of this hill into small plots and let them at a low rent; but the people are poor and their improvements are not substantial.[4]

Lord *Deskfoord*, known as the "Mad Earl", was prone to "fits". When he felt a fit coming-on he locked himself in the Library and dropped the key out of the window to his Factor who released him when he had recovered. One day, in 1766, the Factor, Alexander Grant, released the Laird too soon and was chased up the *Pink Staircase* into an attic room where he was stabbed to death. No charges were brought against Lord *Deskfoord*. The attic room with its blood-stained floor remained unused by the Seafield family until an exorcist was brought in to rid the *Pink Staircase* and the room of an alleged ghost. Years earlier, on 29 July 1738, Lord *Deskfoord* was the only witness to the drowning of Lord Banff, with whom he went swimming in the sea at Black Rocks, Cullen. Did a "mad fit" also play a role in this mysterious death?[6]

On Saturday 3 November 1770 Lord *Deskfoord* took his own life by slashing his wrists.[7] The Aberdeen Journal of Monday 5 November 1770 referred only to "the melancholy accounts of the death of the Earl of Seafield."[8]

Lord *Deskfoord* was succeeded by his only surviving child, James (1750-1811). The new 7th Earl of Findlater, 4th Earl of Seafield had been educated at Oxford. Soon after inheriting the titles the Earl went to live on the Continent. In 1799, in Brussels, he married Christina Teresa Murray, daughter of Joseph Count Murray, Lieutentant-General in the armies of the Emperor of Germany. The couple, who had no issue, soon parted. The Earl died in 1811 in Dresden, where he had gone to hide from a blackmailer. Being last of the Ogilvy line the titles of Findlater and Viscountcy of Seafield thereby expired.[1]

Sir Lewis Alexander Grant(1767-1840), Baronet, cousin of the 4th Earl of Seafield, became 5th Earl, in 1811; he also assumed the surname, Ogilvie. Note the change of spelling. Colonel Francis William Ogilvie-Grant (later 6th Earl) managed the estate for his brother, Sir Lewis, who was unable to handle his own affairs. From 1820, during the lifetime of the 5th and 6th Earls, the new town of Cullen was built, this time nearer the sea, but more importantly for the Earls of Seafield, further away from their family mansion![2]

During the next one hundred years, until 1911, when James Ogilvie-Grant succeeded to the title of 11th Earl of Seafield, none of the title-holders from the 6th to the 10th Earls could lay claim to any special distinguishing qualities for the history books, although Francis William Ogilvie Grant (1778-1853), who succeeded his brother, Sir Lewis, as 6th Earl, was a Representative Peer for Scotland from 1841 to 1853.[1]

James, 11th Earl of Seafield, was 30th Chief of the Clan Grant and a Captain in the 3rd Bn. Queen's Own Cameron Highlanders. In World War I, on 12 November 1915, the 11th Earl died of wounds in action; he was succeeded by his only child, Nina Caroline Ogilvie-Grant, at the tender age of nine years, as Countess of Seafield (12th holder).[2]

In 1930 the Countess married Derek Herbert Studley-Herbert who, in 1939, added Ogilvie-Grant to his name. On Monday 20 March 1939 we could see from our home, the massive Bin Hill bonfire, lit to announce the birth of a son and heir. The Countess and her husband divorced in 1957; he died in 1960, the Countess in 1969.[1]

Ian Derek Francis Ogilvie Grant became the 13th Earl of Seafield in 1969. In 1960 he married Mary Dawn McKenzie Illingworth, by whom he had two children,the Hon. James Andrew Ogilvie-Grant, Viscount Reidhaven and Master of Seafield, born November 1963 who will inherit the title of 14th Earl of Seafield, and the Hon. Alexander Derek Henry Ogilvie-Grant, born 1966; but in 1971 the marriage was dissolved. The Earl married Leila Refaat, daughter of Mahmoud Refaat of Cairo.[1]

Cullen House, the Ogilvy family residence since 1602, had extensive alterations done to it over the succeeding two and a half centuries:James Ogilvy (1664-1730), 4th Earl of Findlater and 1st Earl of Seafield, had the east wing extended in 1711. His grandson, James, 6th Earl of Findlater and 3rd Earl of Seafield, commissioned the famous Adam brothers, James and William, in 1767, to further enhance the house and gardens. John Charles, 7th Earl of Seafield, in 1858, commissioned David Bryce to make further alterations and additions, to create a 386-room mansion, making Cullen House one of the grandest residences in Scotland.[8]

But times change: the 13th (unlucky?) Earl of Seafield, whose birth was marked by the Bonfire, and who inherited the title in 1969, decided to sell-off Cullen House in 1984. It was then converted into eleven separate flats. Two years later, in 1986, this one-time grand family mansion was badly damaged by fire. It has since been rebuilt.[9]

While the Ogilvy's can trace their family history back to the Earl of Angus, in the reign of King David I in the first half of the twelfth century, the Deskford connection began in the fifteenth century, in 1436, when Margaret, heiress of Sir John Sinclair, then proprietor of Deskford, married Sir Walter Ogilvy of Auchleven, in Garioch, Aberdeenshire.

It is not clear when the Ogilvy family took up residence in Deskford but they ceased occupation of the Tower of Deskford by the end of the sixteenth century and it remained unoccupied until the 1830s when its ruins were demolished due to their becoming a danger to the adjoining Established Church, the former St John's Chapel of pre-Reformation times.[5]

Above: ST JOHN'S CHURCH, built in 1871

Left: SACRAMENT HOUSE, 1551: preserved
         in the ruins of St John's Chapel

5

THE KIRK

My ancestors certainly had cause to fear the power of the Kirk and its Elders two centuries ago; swingeing penalties were paid by them for indulging in *fornication*. In the eighteenth and nineteenth centuries, the Kirk wielded immense power over their parishioners: baptism, marriage and burial rites, were all dependent on their obeying its ethics.[1]

The Deskford Kirk Session Minutes date from 1684. An entry dated 17 October 1784, reads:

James Clarke, younger, of Raemore [first born of my gt gt gt Grandparents, James and Elspet] confessed to fornication with Janet Donald.[1]

At the next meeting of the Kirk Session, on 13 November:

Janet paid 2/6d [12.5p], and James £1.11/- [£1.55].

Again, on 19 May 1791:

Walter Clarke [James's younger brother] confessed to antenuptial fornication with Anne Scott and paid 10/- [50p].

Walter married Anne soon after.[1]

The Minutes of 29 June 1806, record that:

James Clarke [again!] confessed, with Lilias Hood, to having a child in fornication; and this being a quadri-lapse in fornication, the case was being referred to the Presbytery of Fordyce, for advice.[1]

In addition, at the same hearing, James was asked:

to pay-up for a penalty imposed earlier, for a tri-lapse in fornication, this time withAnn Dawson. Ann paid 10/- [50p], James £4.00, and were absolved.[1]

22

James married Lilias Hood on 24 August 1806, after paying £2 for his quadri-lapse. Setting these penalties in perspective: two centuries ago a top ploughman earned from £6 to £7 **per year**. So, James paid dearly for his peccadilloes! Ann's 10/-(50p) was equivalent to four month's wages for her.[1]

Most fornicators, when arraigned before the Elders, confessed. The Minutes, however, record a case where gossip hinted at a girl's guilt, which she denied, but she then had to suffer the indignity of being examined (in the presence of the Elders) by a midwife:

squeezing her breasts to check for presence of milk.[!][1]

In other cases where alleged fornicators had fled the parish, the minister was instructed to write to the minister of the other parish in order to bring the miscreants to retribution.[1]

Fornication was not the only offence meriting the Elders' attention: A Minute of 3 July 1825, records:

That James Clarke, [no! his eldest son this time!] of Hoggie, along with three others, was accused of disorderly and riotous behaviour on Sunday 10 June.[1]

The four of them got off with:

an exhortation to repentance and to read selected passages of the Bible.[1]

The *rioting* James in trouble again, on 9 March 1834:

James Clarke was accused of fornication with Mary Booth.

Mary paid 10/-[50p] and was absolved.[1]

James flatly refused to fork out, although he changed his mind three weeks later, when he offered to pay £1.13.4 [£1.67], but the Elders refused to absolve him. Just over three months later, on the 19 July 1834, James appeared before the Elders:

craving to be absolved and agreeing to pay the balance due.[1]

Most fornicators married shortly after, often before the birth of their child. Scotland in the nineteenth century had a higher rate of illegitimacy than England. In the 1860s, Banffshire, compared with other Scottish counties, had the highest illegitimacy rate at nearly seventeen per cent. Crofters were worse than seamen, for reasons unknown. Where the parents of a bastard bairn got married afterwards, the child is legitimate under Scottish Law; English Law differs.[2]

The earliest recorded Church in Deskford was St John's Chapel, which adjoined the southern wall of the Tower of Deskford. Built into an inside wall was a Sacrament House (aumbry) dated 1551, although the Chapel would pre-date that. After the Reformation, in 1560, St John's became the Established Church. Three centuries later, in 1871, a new St John's Church was erected about a quarter of a mile away, by the side of the Keith to Cullen road. This is now the one and only Church for the parishioners of Deskford.[3]

The old Church, now within the Churchyard walls, is roofless, although all four walls still stand. The Sacrament House remains intact, preserved by a perspex cover. In pre-Reformation times the Sacrament House served as a recess to hold the bread, wine and oil used in Catholic Ceremonies.

The aumbry is carved in freestone and depicts two angels supporting the monstrance, bordered with vines and other ornamentation, with the recess underneath. Immediately above the recess is carved the following inscription in Latin:

Os mevm es et caro mea.

(Thou are my bone and my flesh)[Genesis 29:14]

And under the recess there is carved the following:

Ego svm panis vivvs qui de coelo descendi,

(I am the living bread which came down from heaven)

Si quis mandvcaverit ex hoc pane vivet

(if any man eat of this bread, he shall live)

in eternum. Johanis sexto et cetera.

(forever. John V1, etc) [v.51]

Underneath this inscription are the coats of arms of Alexander Ogilvy and that of his second wife, Elizabeth Gordon, with the following words, in Scots:

This pnt [present] loveble vark of Sacrament hous maid to ye honor and lovig of God be ane noble man Alexander Ogilvy of yt ilk and Elizabeth Gordon, his spouse, the yeir of God, 1551.[3]

This Sacrament House is unique in north-east Scotland, being the only one with an inscription in Scots. It is preserved under the Ancient Monuments Protection Act.[3]

In 1543 the *Capella de Deskfurde* or Chapel of Deskford, became the *Ecclesiae de Deskfurde*, i.e. a parish by itself, separate from Fordyce, to which it formerly belonged. Fordyce was too remote for attendance by the people of Deskford and besides there were far too many for one pastor. The two parishes were re-united in 1650, but severed again in 1654.[3]

The Kirkton Churchyard (where the Sacrament House is preserved) contains the remains of many of my ancestors from two centuries back; it is still in use in 1992. It is reputed that Mary Beaton and her husband were buried here sometime after 1606. Mary, in 1566, married Alexander Ogilvy of Boyne Castle, 1.3 miles(2km) east of Portsoy, but is best remembered as one of the Queen's *four Maries*. The *four Maries* accompanied the six-year-old Queen Mary to France in 1548 as the prospective bride of the Dauphin Francis whom she married in 1558 and who became King of France in 1559; he died in December 1560 and Mary returned to Scotland in 1561.[4]

Following the Reformation, Deskford Church did not have a minister for three years. In *Fasti Ecclesiae Scoticanae* the first reference to Deskford is for the year 1563:

William Lawtie, M.A., minister of Banff had also charge here until 1568.[5]

Deskford was made a separate ecclesiastical parish in 1627, making it eligible for a full-time minister. A Rev Walter Darg, M.A., King's College, Aberdeen, was presented by Lord Deskford in 1627. However, he was suspended in 1650, deposed for inefficiency in 1651, silenced by the Synod in 1652, and finally excommunicated by the Presbytery, in 1653.[5]

The Rev Walter Ogilvy took over in 1654, and when he died, he was commemorated by a lozenge-shaped stone monument set into the Church wall near to the Sacrament House which had been built a century earlier. The Latin inscription reads:

Mr Walter Ogilvy, a pious minister in the work of God, now one of the happy inhabitants of Heaven, died 15 February 1658.[6]

The ruined walls of St John's Chapel of pre-Reformation days still stand but no trace exists of The Tower of Deskford which abutted it. The ruins are now within the Kirkton Churchyard.

Because of poverty, the parishioners could contribute very little to the ministers upkeep. To augment the stipend, the Sheriff Clerk of Banffshire, Robert Sharp who married the heiress of Ordens (a farm adjoining ours) made a mortification towards the stipend in 1675. By 1836 this mortification was contributing £1.15.3 (£1.76) annually towards the stipend. Robert Sharp is believed to be the brother of James Sharp, the Archbishop of St Andrews who was murdered in 1679.[7]

Other ministers were appointed, in 1659, 1679 and 1680 respectively. In 1684, a James Henderson, M.A. was presented by the 3rd Earl of Findlater, but in 1689 he was deposed for not reading *The Proclamation of the Estates* to support the *Revolution* when the Scottish Convention offered the crown to the Protestant William and Mary of Orange.[7]

Ten years elapsed before the next minister, the Rev John Murray, took over as replacement; he died in 1719. From 1720 until his death in 1730 the incumbent was the Rev Alexander Philip. In 1731, James, 5th Earl of Findlater and 2nd Earl of Seafield presented the Rev Walter Morrison who served until his death in 1780, when the Rev Walter Chalmers took over. The Rev Walter Chalmers, writing about the Church in 1799, said:

> There is no date upon the church; one pew in it bears 1627, another 1630 and like the generality of churches in this country, is gloomy and miserably furnished.[8]

The Manse, built in 1783, also came in for some criticism:

> The heritor gave a liberal allowance, indulged the incumbent [Rev Walter Chalmers] with his own plan, and every accommodation he could define; and had the undertaker done his duty, it would have been, perhaps, a model of abundant and genteel accommodation; but the work, in every department, is insufficiently executed.[8]

The Reformation brought change to the management of the Kirk, a degree of democracy through annually elected (later, life appointed) lay officers called Elders to form a Kirk Session which met, usually monthly, under the chairmanship of the minister, known as the Moderator. Their decisions were minuted by the Session Clerk, who was usually the Schoolmaster. Another post held by the Schoolmaster was precentor who led the singing of hymns in the Kirk. The duties of the Kirk Session were: to manage the fabric of the Kirk; to disburse poor relief; and to uphold discipline.

In the Disruption of 1843 the Rev George Innes, walked out, taking with him the Kirk Session (less one Elder, James Mitchell, Knowes) and the majority of his parishioners. They set up a Free Kirk, free from the control and influence of the Laird who then had the power to select the minister, the raison d'etre of the Disruption. The Rev George Innes aged 66, preached in a barn for the first year until they built their own Free Kirk. He wrote-up a record of the events as they affected the Parish before he died in 1851. A copy is in the National Library, Edinburgh.[3]

The Rev George Innes, after only fourteen years as minister of the Established Kirk of Deskford, must have been proud of such loyalty from his parishioners, particularly in an era when the power and influence of the Laird was so great.

The Rev James Mackintosh from the adjacent parish of Ordiquhill was presented by Francis William Ogilvie Grant, 6th Earl of Seafield in 1843 to replace the Rev George Innes. When the Rev James Mackintosh died in 1890 his family paid for two stained-glass windows to be fitted to St John's Church as a memorial to their parents.[3]

The Rev George Mathieson Park (B.D. 1889 Aberdeen) took over in 1890 and retired in May 1931 aged 73. Three months later, The West (Free) Kirk united with St John's Church. St John's, (built in 1871 at a cost of £1,000) is now the only church in Deskford. In 1948, the Free Kirk, along with its manse and hall, were sold-off as private dwellings. St John's Church manse, rebuilt in 1873, has also been sold-off as a private dwelling. Today, a fortnightly service is conducted by the minister from Cullen Church. So the Church of Deskford, having once again only the services of a part-time minister, has come full circle in the space of four centuries.[3]

The Church has long lost the immense power and influence which it wielded when my ancestors came to Deskford in 1771. Nowadays, we look back with scorn at the Kirk's fascination with fornication, and at their vain attempt to safeguard the morals of their parishioners. Where has it all got us - or the Kirk, for that matter.

In 1932 when I stayed with Granny Christie in her but-and-ben I remember her explaining to me the meaning of the religious-theme picture, *The Broad and Narrow Way*, hanging above the fireplace. The broad, easy way of life was to indulge in dancing, drinking, gambling, and travelling on Sunday trains; or one was free to take the hard and narrow road to God, through Christianity, by abstemious living and resisting the temptations of dancing, drinking and gambling.

Unlike my ancestors of two centuries ago, I did not go in fear of the Kirk - in fact I never darkened its door! My Brothers John and Ernest and Sister Madge went to Sunday school in the 1920s. However, Madge, aged twelve in 1924, failed to get a prize for perfect attendance even though she had not missed a Sunday. Our Mother, with her volatile temperament, exploded angrily - none of the family ever went to church again. Maybe Mother was still smarting at the ministers involvement with the Will in 1910 which disinherited our Father. Issues rankled long with Mother; two centuries after Culloden, Mother would tremble with anger at the very mention of the Duke of Cumberland and his English soldiers!

After the war I read books on religion, agnosticism and atheism. I also read the Rubaiyat of Omar Khayyam, the Persian philosopher of nine centuries past. Two of his quatrains have reflected my thoughts on religion over the past half century:

> Myself when young did eagerly frequent
> Doctor and Saint, and heard great argument
> About it and about: but evermore
> Came out by the same door where in I went.

> And that inverted Bowl they call the Sky,
> Whereunder crawling coop'd we live and die,
> Lift not your hands to It for help - for It
> As impotently moves as you or I.9

DESKFORD SCHOOL, first built in 1876: now a Community Centre

6

THE TEACHERS

Until the mid-seventeenth century education was mainly provided by the Church. In 1496 The Scottish Parliament passed an Education Act making it:

> compulsory for men of substance to send their eldest son to school to learn Latin, arts and law.[1]

This meant sending their sons to University. Scottish Universities were founded comparatively early: St Andrews (1412), Glasgow (1451), Kings College, Aberdeen (1495), Edinburgh (1583), and Marischal College, Aberdeen (1593).[1]

James Ogilvie, 3rd Earl of Findlater, sent his sons, Walter, James and Patrick, to Marischal College. Before the two Aberdeen Colleges merged in 1860 to form the University, there was rivalry between Marischal College(in the New *Toun*) and Kings College(in the Old *Toun*). The Principal of Marischal College wrote to James Ogilvie, 3rd Earl of Findlater, on 25 April 1692:

> Right Honoble,
>
> Among your troubles I give you, I presume to wreit something in ffavour of your Alma Mater. Mr Alex. Moir, on [one] of the Regents of the Newtoun College, having the Bejane Class [1st year students] this year,is lyk the Important [Importunate] Sturdie Beggars, using all methods to gett Schollers. Among the rest, he has hopes of some ffrom your toun of Cullen - viz. the sone of Bailzie Aird. And if you have any Influence that way (qch I doubt not you have), it will do him a singular kyndness if you recommend him, or at least if your affair wt the old toun Colledge hinder that, ye would not concern yourself(if ye should be Importuned by any of the Masters of the old toun Colledge) agnst him, I hop ye will pardone my using this ffreedom, forr I am,
>
> Right Honobl,
> your most obliged and humble servt., WM.BLACK.[2]

27

Universities in those days were of little consequence to ordinary folk; only Lairds and wealthy farmers could afford to send their sons there. The Scottish Parliament in their 1633 Education Act set out that there **should** be a school in every parish, but nothing much happened. A further Education Act, in 1646, transferred responsibility for schools, from Bishops to Presbyteries. Whether, or not, a school was set up depended very much on the interest of the Laird. Parishes had no money, either to lease land, build a school, or pay a teacher's salary. An Act that said **should**, not **must**, was a pious proposition - and as such utterly useless![1]

Deskford became a separate electoral parish in 1618, but it was not until 1654 that the first schoolmaster, George Lesley, was appointed. George Lesley, who came from Fife, had held teaching posts there and in Mortlach. However, by 1655 he had left to become Schoolmaster in Botriphnie School(where, today, incidentally, a cousin of mine, Mrs Davina Gray holds the post of Head Teacher). A William Gardiner then took over the post, and in 1676, following a visit of the Presbytery, he was being highly commended, as the Presbytery Minutes show:

> There was ane honest man named William Gardiner of a blaimless conversatione, who did precent in the church and was clerk of the session and taught children to read English and wreat, but had little benefits by reason of the meanness of the place and the poverty of the people.[3]

The next reference to a schoolmaster was in 1687 during the ministry of the Rev James Henderson, who was presented in 1684 by the 3rd Earl of Findlater but deposed in 1689 for failing to pray for the new (Protestant) monarchy of William and Mary. However, two years before he was deposed, the Rev James Henderson complained to the Laird:

> That there was not a Grammar School in the parioch [parish]; but one James Sinklair who is of good life, taught English and precented in the church, and had but small encouragement therefor be reason of the poverty of the tenants.[3]

Here was a second reference, within the space of eight years, to the poverty of the people.[3]

It isn't clear how long Mr Sinklair lasted in Deskford. In 1724 the Rev Alexander Philip intimated:

> That he had neither schoolmaster, session clerk, schoolhouse, nor salary; that on severall occasions represented the want of these to the [4th] Earl of Findlater...but that nothing was done.[3]

The 4th Earl of Findlater was the one deeply involved in politics; no doubt he spent a lot of his time in London. In the following year the Presbytery of Fordyce:

> Was able to persuade [4th] Earl Findlater to have a schoolhouse built and to settle a salary of 100 merks [£16, Scots] on a schoolmaster.[3]

Whatever the reasons, schoolmasters did not stay long in Deskford: in the twenty-eight years between 1726 and 1754 the Parish School had gone through a total of ten schoolmasters!

There was also mention of a Dame's school in Berryhillock village in 1735.[3]

Schoolmasters usually also held two other posts: Precentor in the church, and Clerk to the Kirk Session. The Kirk Session Minutes date from 5 November 1684 though with some gaps (1687-94 and 1731-34). Also, in 1751 the Clerk told the Elders:

that having left them [the Minutes] on a shelf in the school closet, as usual, the mice or rats had destroyed some of them from 5 November 1750 to now.[4]

In the next half century, until 1806, there were seven schoolmasters and in 1786:

one of whom fled the country without confession of guilt and another was dismissed after a few months.[3]

A continuing saga of disaffection with Deskford.

In 1806, George Wright was appointed and stayed for thirty-nine years! From 1845 a different method of appointment was adopted: The Rev James Mackintosh (appointed after the Disruption of 1843) met with Mr John Wilson, Factor to the Earl of Seafield, to consider applications for the post of schoolmaster. They resolved to appoint Francis William Grant, a native of Boyndie. Mr Grant left five years later, in 1850. However, in 1851 he was presented by the Earl of Seafield to the pastoral charge of Knockando Kirk, where he died, in 1855.[3] Mr Grant was replaced as minister by my gt Granduncle the Rev John Clarke, until his death in 1866.[5]

I uncovered something of a mystery whilst tracing details of my gt Granduncle John Clarke and his wife, Jane Sinclair, nee Smith. Their third child's birth on 20 June 1855 was registered as *Jane Mariah Sinclair Clarke*, but a note dated 5 November 1855, appended to the birth certificate, said:

the name has been changed, to Caroline Stuart Clarke.

Speculating on reasons for this change, I devised two theories: firstly, that gt Granduncle John, when registering his daughter's birth, had absentmindedly named her after the wrong grandmother or, secondly, that since the manse was near to Cardhu malt whisky distillery he had over-imbibed!

Mentioning this to Mr George Dixon, Archivist for Central Regional Council, he suggested a more plausible explanation. Reaching for his *Fasti Ecclesiae Scoticanae* he noted that the Rev John Clarke had been presented on 6 July 1855 (just two weeks after the birth of his third child) by Sir John Charles Ogilvie-Grant, 7th Earl of Seafield. Turning to Burkes Peerage, Mr Dixon confirmed what he already knew - the Countess of Seafield was called - *Caroline Stuart*!

Mr Dixon suggested that the re-naming was a "special kind of thankyou"; others, might well have uttered, "What a creep!"

In 1836 Deskford had two schools: the parochial school in Kirkton and a Dame's School in Berryhillock which was run by two sisters. The Dame's school had 28 pupils; the fees were:

reading only: two shillings(10p) per quarter; and two shillings and sixpence (12.5p) for reading, sewing and knitting.[6]

The parochial schoolmaster received an annual salary of £32. Subjects taught were reading, writing, English grammar, arithmetic and, when required, Latin. Annual Fees ranged from ten shillings(50p) to £1, if Latin was required. In addition, there were a number of Sabbath Schools in outlying areas.[6]

The Free Kirk started a school for girls in 1844 and one for boys in 1847. Another school for girls was built by public subscription in 1860, in Kirkton. All of these closed in 1876 when the State school opened. The former Kirkton girls school was turned into a lodging-house for women teachers continuing as such until the late 1930s, I believe.[7]

Stability of schoolmasters in Deskford came, in 1868, with the appointment of Mr William Smith who held the post for forty years, until his retirement in December 1908. Mr Smith graduated M.A. in 1863 at Kings College, Aberdeen; he was known, affectionately, as *The Dominie*. An influencing factor in his long stay may have been the building of the new State school in 1876 , eight years after his appointment. This was the first State school in Deskford in accordance with the Education Act, 1872. The school cost £1,182, seated 162 pupils and replaced all existing schools.[3]

The new school was mysteriously burnt down during the night of 18 January 1899, yet was rebuilt in just nine months, by 16 October - surely a record and one to which today's builders might aspire! During rebuilding, the schoolmaster and his two lady teachers used the Church across the road, apparently losing only one week of schooling.[3]

Quite a number of Dominie Smith's pupils became university graduates; probably the most notable would be Ashley Watson Mackintosh, last born, 8 April 1868, of a family of eleven, of the Rev James Mackintosh, minister. Ashley became Professor of Medicine at Aberdeen University and Honorary Physician to the King, when in Scotland, as well as being knighted. My Father, born in 1871, was a fellow scholar with Ashley Mackintosh. At Dominie Smith's retirement in 1908, mention was made of gifts from former pupils including those from my Uncle James, a Glasgow businessman who, of course, attended school along with my Father and Ashley Mackintosh.[3]

A Dominie of my own school days was John A. Beveridge (*JAB*, to us) It was *JAB* who persuaded me to continue my studies at Buckie High School after becoming Dux of Deskford School in 1938. I mentioned earlier that *JAB* was an innovator: he asked me whether or not I wanted the usual inscribed Dux medal, or instead, an inscribed wrist watch. I chose the watch. I used it throughout my RAF career. I still have it, and I treasure it as a very happy memory of my Deskford school days.

All our family attended this school between 1915 and 1945. The rebuilt school was extended in 1939 and again in 1949. Up until 1949 the school toilets were earth-closets which stank to high heaven! The farmer of Squaredoch manured his land with the waste. Come to think of it those peas we pinched from the fields next to the school did taste rather special!

Alas, the school is now a Community Centre; all Deskford schoolchildren are bussed to schools outside the parish, the Juniors to Cullen and some Seniors to Keith. The Parish Hall, erected in 1923, is now a store-room for that modern-day post-war business - the ubiquitous double glazing windows firm!

Gone forever is the sound of the happy and lively laughter of bairns at play; no more to see them lining-up in restless rows at the insistent clangour of the school-bell recalling them from play; no need now to ask for whom the bell tolls - *it tolls for Deskford*!

HOWE O' DESKERT: overlooking Hoggie and School to Bin Hill

7

FARMS AND FOLK

For more than six centuries farming and related work has been the main occupation for most Deskford folk. Quite a few of the farm names in use today date back many centuries. Mention was made earlier of Ardoch and Skeith which existed in 1325 or earlier.[1] From my youth I recall a ditty naming the Deskford farms straddling the Keith to Cullen road, which went:

Clochmacreich and Langlanburn,
Craibstone and Raemore,
Burnheads and Squaredoch,
Moss-side and Ardoch,
Netherblairock and the Clune,
Brankanentham and the Broom.

The last two farms are outside the boundary of Deskford parish, but were probably included to complete the rhyme.

Early examples of farm names can be found in The Annals of Cullen: 961-1904: I give the year of first mention in the Annals and its name, then [with today's spelling in brackets]:

1521, Easter Skeith [part of Skeith]; 1531, Ordecowy [Ardiecow];1541, Echinaltry [Inaltry]; 1545, Knowis [Meikle Knowes]; 1562, Clochmacreich, the only Deskford name of Gaelic origin; 1586; Leitchestown; 1587, Aitthillock [Oathillock]; 1587, Ower Blaraycht [Upper Blairock]; 1588, Squaredoch, and Clunehill.[2]

A further list of farms, dated 1746, comes from the:

Copy of Proof, led by James [5th] Earl of Findlater and [2nd Earl of] Seafield upon a Commission from the Lords of Session (for proving what Lands and Heritages he was possessed of in the year 1745).[3]

Proving the Earl's ownership arose because of the destruction of title deeds when Cullen House was plundered by Bonnie Prince Charlie's Highlanders on 9 April 1746. From the deposition of the Earl's Factor, Alexander Grant, we note:

The kirklands of Deskfoord, manor place, tower, fortalice, the towns [farms] of, Over Blerock [Upper Blairock],Miltoun of Deskfoord, with the corn-mill thereof...lands of Clochmacreich, Over Skeith [Upper Skeith, today merged with Mid Skeith], Craibstone, Croftgloy, Squaredoch, Oathillock, Ordens, Inaltry, Meikle and Little Knowes, Nether Clune and Clunehill [merged with Clunehill], Leitchestown, Raemore, lands of Skeith and the mill thereof. That the tenants of Findlater have universally been in use of casting peats in Altmore [Aultmore].[3]

The following farms, not mentioned in 1746, appear in the earliest existing Cullen House rent-roll for Deskford, dated 1766: Hoggie (tenanted by my gt gt Granduncle James from 1806) and the nearby farms of Hollanbush, Broadrashes, Green Hill, Kintywards, Upper Broadrashes, Backies and Langlanburn. Some of these no longer exist, having been merged with other farms.[4] Records show a meal mill at Millton, a tiny village in the north of the parish, in 1745.[3]

A meal mill at Berryhillock in 1836, was mentioned. This mill and its two dams (filled from the Deskford Burn) together with the village were created about 1800.[5]

In 1869 Robert Cruickshank purchased the Berryhillock mill. Fifty years later in 1919 he left it to his son-in-law, Stanley Baldwin. At Stanley Baldwin's retirement party in May 1957 William Currie, farmer, Green Hill, confided that the locals had given Stanley (a grocer in Kent before his call-up for the 1914-18 War) about six months before turning-tail for England - he stayed for thirty-nine years! A Mr George Clark (no relation), from Cullen purchased this mill in 1957 and kept it going until May 1965 with my Brother John as miller completing for him nearly forty years at the mill.[6]

In 1799 Deskford had 18 weavers, 8 shoemakers, 4 tailors, 3 masons, and 2 each of blacksmiths, wrights,wheelwrights,cartwrights and ploughwrights.[7]

One job not mentioned, apart from farm workers, was that of gamekeeper. The *gamie*, as we called him, sought to deter poachers and generally to manage game on the Laird's land ready for the Grouse Shoot on 12 August or around Christmas when the Laird's cronies would assemble at Aultmore Lodge for a shooting spree. A nice little earner for the Earl!

The gamekeeper at the Lodge was James Maitland who married Isabella Clarke my Grandaunt from Mid Skeith, in 1863. By 1883 James and Isabella had saved up enough to take on the tenancy of Raemore. He farmed there until his death in 1914. His son, James took over and continued farming there until 1933.[4]

The Rev George Innes scathingly referred to a commercial venture in Deskford, in 1836:

though the number of alehouses be reduced, there is still one, which is quite unnecessary and affords facilities and temptations to intemperance.[8]

Scotland in the early nineteenth century did consume a lot of whisky: in the 1830s the population aged fifteen and over was drinking, each week, just under a pint each of duty-charged whisky.That statistic excluded illegally made whisky.[9]

An article in the Banffshire Advertiser of 18 June 1896 entitled, *The Old Smuggling Days*, recalls the events:

Fines for smuggling were formerly small, but about 1825, three Deskford crofters were fined £20 each and since one could not pay the fine he was sent to jail. Some six or eight farmers used to join together to bear the expense of purchasing a whisky pot. These pots were, of course, hidden away. One day, Geddes, the gauger came upon a pot and took it to Berryhillock, but no one was willing to claim it. "Na! Na!, they said, we dinna deal wi' that."[10]

To warn of the approach of a gauger, the locals had:

a well understood system of signals; Betty Dougal from the height opposite Squaredoch, hoisted a sheet...soon the news was telegraphed from point to point till it spread all over the parish. An ingenious device[ploy] once saved the farmer of Mid Skeith [my gt gt Grandfather, Alexander Clarke]. Betty Dougal's sheet was hoisted and he had an exceptionally large quantity of malt [taxed from 1713]. He filled a number of sacks with the malt, carted them off to the field and, since it was seed-time, placed them at intervals over the field. Needless to say, the gauger didn't find the malt![10]

About a dozen other jobs were created when Tochieneal Distillery (malt whisky) was set up in 1824 by Alexander Wilson who farmed the 52-acre(21 hectare) Tochieneal farm. Alexander was also Factor to the 5th Earl of Seafield. He was the third of four Wilsons who held the prestigious post of Seafield Estates Factor between 1766 and 1852.[11]

The first Wilson, also called Alexander, began the *dynasty* in 1766 when he succeeded Alexander Grant, the Factor maltreated by Prince Charlie's Highlanders in 1746 when they ransacked Cullen House and who was stabbed to death by his employer, Lord *Deskfoord*, in 1766. Alexander served until 1785, after which his brother John was appointed, serving until 1812. John Wilson was then succeeded by **his** nephew, Alexander (the one starting the distillery). In 1831, Alexander's nephew, John Wilson took over, until 1852. Four Wilsons in eighty-six years - looks like nepotism run riot![11]

John Wilson was an astute businessman since, in 1841 he took advantage of the clay deposited on his farm ten thousand years earlier by the Ice Age and started a Tileworks. Initially, the Tileworks made drain pipes but later, turned-out roof tiles, bricks, chimney cans and flower-pots. The Tileworks supplied farmers, including the Seafield Estates, for their extensive drainage schemes on Deskford farms.[11]

A *lordship* for minerals extracted and sold had to be paid to the Laird. For tiles the levy was sixpence (2.5p) per one thousand items and in 1865 the Laird received £25 for this alone! John Wilson also paid a *lordship* for his Whitehouse Peat Moss. Craibstone Quarries also stumped-up their levy. Another nice little earner for the Earl - for doing nothing![11]

A fifth Wilson, John's brother Sandy, took over as Factor for the Cullen area only in 1852 under Mr William G Bryson, main Factor, but resigned in 1853 due to differences with John Charles Ogilvie-Grant, 7th Earl of Seafield.[11]

In 1871, Sandy Wilson closed the Tochieneal Distillery. This was probably due to a doubling of his rent the previous year and to continuous sniping by the Countess of Seafield *(Caroline Stuart!)* for having a distillery on Seafield lands. Sandy built a new one at Inchgower near Buckie. Fifty-eight years later, in 1929 Sandy Wilson's nephew sold the Inchgower Distillery to Buckie Town Council who resold it to Arthur Bell, Whisky Distillers of Perth, in 1936.[11]

The earliest population statistic for Deskford comes from the *unofficial* census of Scotland, compiled in 1755 by Dr Alexander Webster, minister of Tolbooth Parish in Edinburgh, who invoked the help of fellow parish ministers. Dr Webster's census showed that Scotland's population in 1755 was 1,265,000, while Deskford's was 940. By 1799 this had dropped to 752 due to: a cut in quarrying limestone at Craibstone to conserve the moss; amalgamations of tiny crofts with nearby farms; and restrictions on sub-letting by tenants, from one to three, depending on farm size.[8] Hoggie, 21 acres (9 hectares), had four sub-tenants when gt gt Granduncle James (1752-1837) took on a tenancy there in 1806.[4]

Deskford's population at the first official Census in 1801 was 610. By 1861 it peaked at 1,031, thereafter declining. By 1931 it was down to 541 and at the 1951 Census, 415. The Census no longer publish parish figures but Grampian Regional Council kindly abstracted the 1991 figures to show a new low of 160![12]

Reasons for the decline were due, mainly to the need for less labour arising from inventions in the mid-nineteenth century of a host of agricultural implements like binders, broadcasters, reapers, threshers and milking-machines.[9]

The depression of the 1920s and the General Strike in 1926 led to labour lay-offs. This was the time of tramps roaming the countryside. Deskford had two: Happy Harry and Meg Pom who tramped separately. Father would allow tramps to sleep in the barn, provided they handed-over their matches. Meg and Harry were harmless souls, victims of uncaring governments.

In the 1930s farm workers' wages were disgracefully low. A top ploughman, at this time at the end of six months hard graft would have been paid £20. In 1899 the amount would have been £15, while a century earlier, in 1799 his six month's wage would have been £3. Second and third horsemen and cattlemen, would all have been paid much less.[13]

Unmarried farm servants slept in a chilly cheerless *chaumer*, going to the farmhouse kitchen for their food - brose for breakfast, tatties and mince or broth with oatcakes for both mid-day and evening meals, and rarely any meat. Such boring regularity of the same fare. No wonder many single men moved to a different farm every six months, doubtless hoping for some marginal improvement from their next employer!

Married men in tied cottar-houses would move annually at the May term. Thankfully, nowadays, farm workers get paid weekly. Tied cottages have all but gone and the notorious feeing markets abandoned. Not before time as they were only a degree different from the slave markets of ages past.

In the 1930s, prices at the cattle mart in Cornhill were so derisory that Father often trudged back home with the stirks unsold - and no money for Mother to buy us food! That was the cruelty of crofting between the wars in north-east Scotland.

The 1930s saw the Knackery lorry regularly removing beasts which had died of the deadly Anthrax. In 1938, the dreaded *grass sickness*, a mystery illness among horses, took its toll. Fortunately our two horses were spared; losing one would have been calamity enough, but two would have been disaster! The loss of so many horses led farmers to buy tractors, further decimating the work-force. World War II hastened this decline.

Ironically, it took World War II to put farming on its feet; home-grown food was back on the table, and between 1945 and 1951 the Labour Governments' policies of subsidies for farms and guaranteed prices at the mart set the money jingling in farmers' pockets. The transformation in farmers' fortunes can best be summed-up in the words of one who boasted that, because of Labour's agricultural policies he could now afford to pay his annual subscription - to the Tory Party!

In the twenty years between the Wars (1919-39) there was a very active Amateur Dramatic Society which put on plays, not only in Deskford Parish Hall but also outside the parish. In fact they were quite well known. Although I was too young to play any part, I always remember our English teacher, Miss Milne, at Buckie High School, commenting on the way I was reading out my part in a play we were doing, and adding:

Ah, but of course, you come from Deskford, famous for its Amateur Dramatics!

I think she meant it as a compliment.

Deskford Mutual Improvement Society formed in 1854 was still meeting a century later and was then believed to be the oldest of its kind in Scotland. Dances, whist drives and plays were performed under its auspices, first in the school and, from 1923, in the Parish Hall. Nowadays, folk can go further afield for their entertainment, being no longer dependent on Harry Tamson's *gramophone recitals*, or the School Concert.

Deskford Horticultural Society held its first Flower Show in 1886. The local paper reported that:

there were nearly 500 entries and 500 people attending, afterwards going to a dance in a barn at Carestown farm until four o'clock next morning.[14]

Dominie Smith acted as the Society's Secretary and succeeding Heads continued the precedent. A show has been held annually since, the only exceptions being during war-time.14

Deskford, today, has two villages, Berryhillock and Kirkton, each a quarter of a mile in opposite directions from the Church and Community Centre, each with a dozen houses. In the 1930s, Berryhillock had two general shops, one with a garage, run by my late Uncle Jimmy Muiry, the other one with the post office run by the Misses Reid sisters. In between was *Dovey* Legge the souter. Two walls of *Dovey's* workshop had bunk seats on which we sat and watched him work. Kirkton village also had a souter, making two in Deskford, compared with eight in 1799.

We would visit Wardleys Smiddy, Berryhillock, to see horses being shod.I used to wince at the thought of a nail penetrating their flesh! This Smiddy along with Cottarton of Ardoch, closed after World War II. There was the carpenter-cum-undertaker, Johnny Gordon, one of the few with a car, so rare, that, sixty years on, I can recall its number: *SO 5801!* Sometimes we would see a coffin, in beautiful, shiny wood.

Around the corner was the meal mill where Brother John was miller for nearly 40 years. The mill has closed down and its two dams filled-in. The two general stores have gone, as have the souters' shops in Berryhillock and Kirkton. Today, in 1992, the entire parish has less than one hundred homes left.

In the 1990s the Common Agricultural Policy (CAP) is causing farmers to feel the pinch; diversification is on the agenda. Even sadder, in a world hungry for food, farmers are being forced to *set-aside* land - and getting paid to do so! Many farmers are being bankrupted and, yet some outsiders have the kind of money to buy up their farms to use for other purposes. One farm has been turned into a fortress hideaway, protected by state-of-the-art security systems, by a foreign financier conducting world-wide deals by computer, behind locked doors and gates. Immigration of *foreigners* is something new to Deskford and over the years it is bound to change its culture.

When gt gt gt Grandfather James Clarke came to Deskford in 1771 the largest farms were about 100 acres (40 hectares); today, the size is nearer to 500 acres (200 hectares). Mid Skeith, which was farmed by Clarkes from 1795 to 1943, was amalgamated with Upper Broadrashes and Little Skeith when their leases expired. Hoggie, farmed by Clarkes from 1806 to 1956 is currently managed by the Seafield Estates.[4]

To facilitate large scale farming with its leviathan cultivators and harvesters, boundary fences, hedges, ditches and dykes are being bull-dozed flat; the farm houses are being let to non-farming folk and the unused steadings left to rot. The thirty-seven family farms existing in the 1930s are slowly disappearing. It has even been suggested that one day Deskford will consist of only **two** farms, one on each side of the Keith to Cullen road, each of about 4,000 acres (1600 hectares)! No single individual could ever raise the capital to finance such huge estates; the anonymous conglomerates taking over will lack the humanity of some of the earlier Earls of Seafield.

Postscript

Today, bereft of its school, teachers, school-children and resident minister, its shops all gone, and ever fewer farming jobs, sadly, but surely, Deskford is destined for the dustbin of history. Individuals can choose to some extent to go their own way, either to follow the herd and do as the majority does or buck the trend of fad and fashion and be different. Yet, I do not think that we can ever escape, entirely, the influence of Lairds and entrepreneurs, or that of the church, or school.

If the Jesuits are right, our early years are the ones where our characters are moulded - for life. However, I doubt that one could ever look at, listen to, or converse with a stranger and say - there goes a *Deskert loon or Deskert quine.*

A few exiles, like myself, will pay an occasional nostalgic visit to a place they loved and left but, unable to recognise a familiar face, will leave again with memories of an age that has gone forever, an age that young folks will never know nor even care about because to them, it is today that matters - not yesterday's history!

References

Chapter 1: From Picts to the Present

1   MacPherson-Grant of Ballindalloch Papers, 2nd Jan.1771,
     Survey No. 771: National Register of Archives (Scotland)
2   2nd Statistical Account, Deskford, 1836
3   W. Cramond, LL.D., The Annals of Cullen: 961-1904, 1904
4   Register of the Great Seal: 1306-1424 (Vol 1)
5   1st Statistical Account, Deskford, 1799
6   T. C. Smout, A History of the Scottish People, 1987
7   The Church of Deskford, Moray District Library
8   The Northern Scot, February 21, 1992.

Chapter 2: The Hungry Thirties

1   Northern Scot, 25 July, 1986
2   Memorial Inscription in Rathven Churchyard

Chapter 3: Inheritance Lost

1   Memorial Inscription in Rathven Churchyard
2   Seafield Estates Archives, S. R. O.
3   Fasti Ecclesiae Scoticanae, 1926
4   Will of Ann Anderson Clarke, 1913, S. R. O.

Chapter 4: The Lairds

1   Burkes Peerage, 1990.
2   W. Cramond, LL.D, The Annals of Cullen: 961-1904, 1904.
3   Michael Lynch, Scotland:A New History, 1991
4   1st Statistical Account, Deskford, 1799
5   2nd Statistical Account, Deskford, 1836
6   Mrs C. A. Ritchie, Cullen House Guide, c.1960.
7   McPherson-Grant of Ballindalloch Papers, 2nd Jan.1771,
     Survey No.771:National Register of Archives (Scotland).
8   Aberdeen Journal, 5 November 1770.
9   Charles McKean, The District of Moray: Illustrated Architectural Guide, 1987

Chapter 5: The Kirk

1   Deskford Kirk Session Minutes, from 1684, S. R. O.
2   T. C. Smout, A Century of the Scottish People, 1987
3   3rd Statistical Account, Deskford, 1957
4   Gordon Donaldson and Robert S. Morpeth, A Dictionary of
     Scottish History, 1988
5   Fasti Ecclesiae Scoticanae, 1926
6   Charles McKean, The District of Moray: Illustrated Architectural Guide, 1987
7   W. Cramond, LL.D., The Annals of Cullen:961-1904, 1904
8   1st Statistical Account, Deskford, 1799
9   Edw. Fitzgerald, Rubaiyat of Omar Khayyam, 5th Edn, 1979

Chapter 6: The Teachers

1   Gordon Donaldson and Robert S. Morpeth, A Dictionary of
     Scottish History, 1988
2   J. Grant, M.A., The Education of a Scots Nobleman:
     200 Years Ago
3   W. Barclay, Schoolmasters of Banffshire, in the
     Banffshire Journal, 1925
4   Deskford Kirk Session Minutes, from 1684, S. R. O.
5   Fasti Ecclesiae Scoticanae, 1926
6   2nd Statistical Account, Deskford, 1836
7   3rd Statistical Account, Deskford, 1957

Chapter 7: Farms & Folk

1   Register of the Great Seal:1306-1424 (Vol 1)
2   W. Cramond, LL.D., The Annals of Cullen: 961-1904, 1904
3   Report by a Commission from the Lords of Session, on
     Copy of Proof led by James [5th] Earl of Findlater and
     Seafield; for proving lands and heritages in 1745.
     Moray District Library, L941.223
4   Seafield Estates Archives, S.R.O.
5   Charles McKean, The District of Moray: Illustrated Architectural Guide, 1987
6   Herald (Farming News), 18 May 1957
7   1st Statistical Account, Deskford, 1799
8   2nd Statistical Account, Deskford, 1836
9   T. C. Smout, A Century of the Scottish People, 1987
10   Banffshire Advertiser, 18 June 1896
11   A. C. Brown, The Wilsons: A Banffshire Family, 1936
12   Grampian Regional Council: Economic & Planning Department
13   3rd Statistical Account, Deskford, 1957
14   Northern Scot, May 1991

Index

Aberdeen vii,13,17,24,27,30
Aberdeen & N.E.S.F.H.Scy. vii
Aberdeen Journal 20
Act of Union 18
Agnosticism 26
Agricultural Improver 19
Aitthillock 31
Aladdins Cave 15
Alehouses 32
Alma Mater 27
Amateur Dramatic Society 35
Ancient Mnmts. Protn.Act 24
Anderson , Alex 1,12
         , Ann 12,14,15
         , Aul' Dod 8
         , James 12
         , John 1,12
Andrew, Elspet 12,13
Angus, Earl of 21
Animal Farm 11
Annals of Cullen 3,31
Anthrax 35
Anti-Communist 11
Archbishop of St Andrews 25
Archivist 29
Ardache 2
Ardiecow 31
Ardoch 2,31
Arts 27
Atheism 26
Auchindoun Castle 17
Auchleven 17
Auld Sang 18
Aultmore 32
         Lodge 32
Australia vii
Backies 32
Bailzie Aird 27
Baldwin, Stanley 32
Banff 24
Banff Institution 1
Banffshire Advertiser 33
Banffshire Journal 11
Banffy 11
Bannocks 9
Barclay,The Rt Rev J.J.J. vii
Barony of Deskford 2,3,17
Beaton, Mary 24
Bejane Class 27
Bell, Arthur 34
Berryhillock 2,4,5,28,29,32,
              33,35
         Mill 32
Beveridge, J. A. 10,30
Binders 34
Bin Hill 2,11

Birrels Chocolates 14
Blackhill 2
Blacksmith 32
Black, William 27
Bleachfield 19
Boar 1
Bogie Roll Tobacco 6
Bonnie Prince Charlie 31,33
Booth, Mary 23
Boswell, James 3
Botriphnie 28
Boyndie 29
Boyne Castle 24
Brankanentham 31
British Government 19
Broad and Narrow Way 26
Broadcaster 34
Broadrashes 32
Broom 31
Bruce, Elizabeth 2
Bruce Henderson Mem. Awrd. vii
Bryson, W. G. 33
Buckie 2,11,34
         High School 10,11,30,35
         Town Council 34
But-and-Ben 14,26
Cairo 21
Canada vii,13
Capella de Deskfurde 24
Cardhu Distillery 29
Carnyx 1
Cartwrights 32
Catholic Ceremonies 23
Census , 1801(Deskford) 34
         , 1891(Grange) 7,15
         , 1951(Deskford) 34
Chair-o-Planes 7
Chalmers, Rev Walter 3,20,25
Chapel of Deskford 17
Charter , 1325 2
         , 1537 4
Chaumer 8,34
Christianity 26
Christie , Isabella 7,14,26
         , Margaret 7,15
         , Sarah Ann McN. 7,15
Church of Deskford 2,21,23-26
Clarke , Allan 16
         , Alex 12-15,33
         , Ann 14
         , Caroline Stuart 29
         , Elspeth(Eppy) 12,15,16
         , Ernest 16,26
         , George 14,16,32
         , Isabella 12,32
         , James(Raemore) 11-13

39

Radio 9
Raemore 11-13,22,31,32
RAF 4,6,30
Ragged Trousrd Phlnthrps.11
Rathven vi,12
        Market 7
Reaper, Margaret 7,15
Red Barn Murder Mystery 11
Red Letter 11
Refaat , Leila 21
        , Mahmoud 21
Reformation, 1560 23,25
Reidhaven, Viscount 18,21
Reid, Misses 6
Rent-roll 32
Revolution, 1917 11
Ritchisone, John 3
Roman Coins 2
        Fort 2
        Legions 1
Rotation of Crops 19
Russell, Barbara 12
Sabbath School 29
Sacrament House 23,24
St Andrews University 27
St John's Chapel 21,23,25
St John's Tree 3
St Mary's Church 2
St Peter's Church 7
Salmonella 9
Salt Tax 19
Sauchiehall Street 14
Scailie 9
School Concert 35
School of Deskford 2,28
Scones 9
Scott, Anne 22
Scottish Convention 25
        Parliament 27,28
Seafield , 1st Earl 18
        , 2nd   19,25,31
        , 3rd   19,21
        , 4th   20
        , 5th   20,33
        , 6th   20,21,26
        , 7th   20,21,29,33
        , 11th   21
        , 12th,Countess 21
        , 13th Earl 21
        , 14th   21
        , Estates 14,20,33,36
        , Street 16
        , Viscountcy 18,20
Seamen 23
Secret Army 4
Secretary of State 18
Session Clerk 25
Set-aside 36

Sharp , James 25
      , Robert 25
Shepherd 16
Shepherd, Isobel 12,13
Sheriff 3
Sheriff Clerk 25
Shoemaker 32
Sinclair   , Alexander 17
          , Margaret 3,12,17,21
          , Sir John 3,17
Sinklair, James 28
Skeith 2,4,31,32
Slate 9
Smiddy 35
Smith   , Alex A. 15
       , Jane Sinclair 29
       , William 30
Smugglers 1
Smuggling Days 33
Social Security 7
Solicitor General 18
Soo 9
Souter 35,36
Sowens 3
Squaredoch 32,33
Star 6
Steinson, Margaret 12
Stem Mull 8
Stephen   , Howard(Howie) 4
         , Joan 4
Stills 1
Stipend 25
Stirling vii
Stirling Open Writing Comp.vii
Stone, Harry 4
Strathislay 4
Studley-Herbert, Derek H. 21
Stuart, Caroline 29,34
Stuart's Records 4
Suicide 1,3,20
Summertown Hill 2
Sunday School 26
Sutherland, James 15
Swan, Annie S. 11
Sway 5
Switzerland vii
Syme, George 3
Synod 24
Syrup 10
Tailors 32
Tamson, Harry 9,35
Tawse 10
Taxation Policies 19
Thermos Flasks 6
Threshers 34
Tilley Lamp 6
Tochieneal Distillery 33,34
        Farm 19,33